DAVID E. LATANÉ, JR.

Browning's *Sordello* and the Aesthetics of Difficulty

English Literary Studies
University of Victoria
1987

© 1987 by David E. Latané, Jr.

ELS Editions
Department of English
University of Victoria
Victoria, BC
Canada V8W 3W1
www.elseditions.com

Founding Editor: Samuel L. Macey

General Editor: Luke Carson

Printed by CreateSpace

English literary studies monograph series
ISSN 0829-7681 ; 40
ISBN-10 0-920604-33-1
ISBN-13 978-0-920604-33-5

For my Father

CONTENTS

It is a modern hieroglyphic, and should be carved on stone for the use of schools and colleges. Professors of poetry should decipher and comment upon a few lines every morning before breakfast, and young students should be *ground* upon it. It is a fine mental exercise."—R. H. HORNE, 1844

you have *made* even the darkness of it!—ELIZABETH BARRETT, 1845

INTRODUCTION

On the 21st of June, 1841, Thomas Carlyle sat down in his study at Chelsea with two volumes of poetry — gifts from the author — and prepared to write a letter. *Sordello* and *Pippa Passes* had greatly impressed him, and he had been acquainted with Robert Browning for some five years. In a friendly way he advised Browning to struggle with the problem of clarity:

> Unless I very greatly mistake, judging from these two works, you seem to possess a rare spiritual gift, poetical, pictorial, intellectual, by whatever name we may prefer calling it; to unfold which into articulate clearness is naturally the problem of all problems for you. This noble endowment, it seems to me farther, you are *not* at present on the best way for unfolding; — and if the world had loudly called itself content with these two Poems, my surmise is, the world could have rendered you no fataller disservice than that same! Believe me I speak with sincerity; and if I had not loved you well, I would not have spoken at all.[1]

Browning by this time was smarting from the failure with the public of his most ambitious work to date, as well as its sequel, *Pippa Passes*, and Carlyle's note of encouragement was to be remembered for the rest of his life. Carlyle's own "quarrel with the Nominative-and-Verb" made his style difficult and controversial, and in forging a poem of enormous difficulty for the reader that failed to impress Carlyle with the correctness of his "way for unfolding" his genius, Browning had misread his audience.[2] Jane Carlyle's jibe that she had read the poem with interest but been unable to discern whether Sordello was a man, a city, or a book was a more typical reaction than Carlyle's tempered praise and blame. *Sordello*'s reputation as an estimable work in its own right (as opposed to an important cog in Browning's development of the monologue, or as a quarry to be mined for statements to support various theses about the monologue) has been slow in coming. The history of its reception may be compared to that of Blake's epics: as critics have used Blake's songs against his prophecies, they have also used the dramatic monologues against *Sordello*, as paratactic examples of how one poet could be both so

9

right and so wrong. It is still not unusual to find statements like the following in books on Victorian poetry: "I make no apologies for my omission of *Sordello*. Jane Carlyle may not have said the last word on that monster, but I shall leave it to others to challenge her judgment."[3] One of the reasons the poem has been considered monstrous, I think, is that it has been from the start judged by a standard of "articulate clearness" when its poetic aim — its deliberate choice of aesthetics — has been towards difficulty. When a critic states that "the language of the poem is often incomprehensible" and that there are "numerous lines which mean nothing," we should remember that if these statements reflect an aesthetics of clarity, nothing of the sort was intended.[4]

Sordello has often been regarded as the ultimate difficult poem, at least until its twentieth-century successors. It is also usually seen as an anomalous freak of literary history. I think that Browning's early masterwork can be understood best, however, as a mature extension of the poetics of its time, as well as a late-Romantic attempt to write an epical work which must be read both willfully and imaginatively. For this reason, in discussing the idea of audience and the effect of poetry in *Sordello*, I have wandered out of the poem and into the context of the decade of the 1830s, whose sense of belatedness (and at the same time, wonder at the rapidity of post-diluvian change) results in a *Zeitgeist* whose characteristics include the fear that the geist is gone, especially from poetry. As Lionel Stevenson remarks, "for young people growing up in the 1820's and feeling an impulse to become poets, the adversaries were too formidable to be ignored. As never before, a poet was obliged to justify his choice of vocation, first of all to himself and thereafter to the readers with whom he hoped to communicate."[5] Browning's poem is not only such a justification but a sophisticated reaction to other contemporary justifications, especially the neo-Coleridgean theology of the poet as internunciate between heaven and earth, and the sharp criticism of the (contemporary) poet implied in Carlyle's writings, even his spiels on the hero as poet or man of letters. I have focussed in particular on the consonance between the work of Browning and his older contemporary Carlyle. Twenty years ago Morse Peckham noted that Carlyle "was Browning's master in an important sense yet to be thoroughly explored," and he pointed to Carlyle's *French Revolution* as the cause of the shift in style from *Paracelsus* to *Sordello*.[6] Much still remains to be done, but I have attempted to make a closer connection between the two in some particulars that have previously gone unnoticed.

Browning's early work, as all critics have noted, is of a piece. *Pauline*,

Paracelsus, *Strafford*, and *Sordello* confront the same problems and argue in related terms. The culminating statement is *Sordello*, which is a model poem for poets who desire a way to continue writing long poems that are viable challengers for the position of honor atop literature's hierarchy of genres. While it has been a temptation to make lengthy excursions into the poems that precede *Sordello*, I have resisted, and have instead contented myself with a look at *Pippa Passes*, a poem that is too little regarded as a product of the 1830s (it was begun before the completion of the decade, if not published until 1841), and seldom seen as a close relative of *Sordello*. In fact, the vicissitudes of reception give the illusion that *Pippa Passes* represents a correction to Browning's poetics after the failure of *Sordello*, whereas I think it plausible to say that *Pippa* would have been exactly the same even if the earlier poem had been an unqualified success with the public and the critics. The main thrust of my argument, however, will be to attempt to display the context necessary for *Sordello*'s creation, in order to study the thematic concerns within the poem relating to this context. Scholarship long ago established that the rhetoric of Romantic poetry forces creative participation between text and reader. What I hope to explore is the particular historical character of this notion as it is available to and reactive upon young writers such as Robert Browning in the 1830s. The easiest way to force greater participation is through an increase in the complexity of style, thought, and figure. A corresponding decrease in the number of readers is made up by their quality. By the 1830s, paradoxically, a new orthodox view that great works must be difficult, obscure, neglected, and ridiculed is so widespread that some works written to this aesthetic — such as *The French Revolution* and *Sartor Resartus* — could become moderately popular. Such was not to be the case with Browning's poem, and the poem itself contains the best analysis of why this should be so.

Browning's ideal of "brother's speech," and the failure of any poet to achieve its communicative absolute, is itself a theme of *Sordello*. It is a language which tests the brother-reader, narrows the audience to the fit though few, and asks us to see an "after-gust" in the making. I shall weigh my interpretation towards the poem's beginning, as well as passages given relatively slight attention, to show how the reader is compelled towards more active reading from the first. But my selective readings are, I hope, examples of how an understanding of the idea of reader-participation, based on an aesthetics of difficulty present in Browning's work and in other writings of the 1830s, may affect our reading of the entire poem. *Sordello*, despite the hope of an "after-gust" at the poem's close, seems to have shut rather than opened the way for the development of the disjunctive epic — at least for the Victorian era. (Despite recent claims, I can't see Tennyson's *In Memoriam* as a radical experiment leading to modernist poetics.) But Browning's unexampled themes, through their impact on Ezra Pound and others, have had a significant though largely untraced influence on the twentieth-century long poem.

Browning himself, when casting about for ways to make money from his poetry in the 1850s, thought of recasting *Sordello* in order to dispel some of the difficulties. While he never fulfilled his promise to change the character of his first masterwork completely, his numerous changes in later editions were designed to make the reader's passage less arduous. Since my subject is the nature of the poetics that shaped *Sordello* as published in 1840, I have taken the unusual step of quoting throughout from the first editions — not only of *Sordello*, but of Browning's other early works as well. All line numbers, however, are from the Ohio Edition of Browning's works, which uses the final collected edition of 1888-89 for its copytext, with variants at the bottom of the page. (*The Complete Works of Robert Browning*, ed. Roma King, et al. 7 vols to date. Athens: Ohio University Press, and Waco, TX: Armstrong Browning Library, 1969.) An earlier version of part of chapter four was previously published in *Victorian Poetry* as "Browning, Byron, and the Revolutionary Deluge in *Sordello*, Book I"; I would like to thank the editors for permission to reprint. My own debt to Browning scholarship is substantial, especially the works of Herbert F. Tucker, Clyde de L. Ryals (whose Browning seminar instigated my interest in the poem), Lawrence Poston and others who recently have explored the terrain of Browning's early career and the context of the 1830s. I am also grateful to the editors of the ongoing editions of the complete letters of Thomas and Jane Welsh Carlyle, and Robert and Elizabeth Barrett Browning. These scholarly editions make many contributions to our understanding of the age beyond the printing of the texts of the letters. In addition, Philip Kelley kindly provided me with a photocopy of the first edition of *Sordello*, and thus insured the accuracy of my quotations, and I wish to offer him my especial thanks. I am also indebted to Robert Gleckner, whose encouragement and interest in my work has helped make me a better scholar. By their detailed suggestions for revision, Boyd Berry of VCU, and the anonymous readers for the ELS Monograph Series, made this a better work, though the defects that remain are, of course, entirely my responsibility. A summer grant-in-aid from Virginia Commonwealth University helped make the completion of this project possible.

List of Works Abbreviated in the Text

(*CW*) — Roma A. King, general editor, *The Complete Works of Robert Browning, With Variant Readings & Annotations*. Vols. 1-3. Athens: Ohio University Press, 1969-1971.

(*Letters*) — T. L. Hood, ed., *Letters of Robert Browning*. London: Murray, 1933.

(*New Letters*) — William Clyde DeVane and Kenneth Leslie Knickerbocker, eds., *New Letters of Robert Browning*. New Haven: Yale University Press, 1950.

(*Letters of RB and EBB*) — Elvin Kintner, ed., *The Letters of Robert Browning and Elizabeth Barrett Browning, 1845-1846*. 2 vols. Cambridge, MA: Belknap Press, 1969.

(*RB & AD*) — Frederic G. Kenyon, ed., *Robert Browning and Alfred Domett*. London: Smith, Elder, & Co., 1906.

(*Correspondence*) — Philip Kelley & Ronald Hudson, eds., *The Brownings' Correspondence*. 3 vols. to date. Winfield, KS: Wedgestone Press, 1984.

(*Works*) — Thomas Carlyle, *The Works of Thomas Carlyle*. 30 vols. Centenery Ed. (London: 1896-1899).

CHAPTER ONE

Reading and the Aesthetics of Difficulty

I

One of the clues to the development of an aesthetics of difficulty may be found in the tensions in Romantic poetry between the popular audience and the coterie of understanders, who take their motto from Milton's line to Urania: "Still govern thou my song, / Urania, and fit audience find, though few" (*PL*, VII, 30-31). One modern critic notes that the phrase is quoted with "astonishing frequency" by the Romantics, and this appeal of Milton's is often found in connection with the idea that, in Walter Scott's phrase, "the 'Paradise Lost' fell still-born from the press."[1] Despite Dr. Johnson's sturdy refutation of this myth, many writers of the Romantic era persisted in the belief that England's greatest epic poet met with utter rejection at the hands of the public, and in their writings they express a desire that their own poems may have a similar fate: that is, an initially small, "fit" audience, followed by the approbation of the ages. Milton's rhetorical stance, halfway through his epic is also important; just before his declaration he says

> ... I sing with mortal voice, unchang'd
> To hoarse or mute, though fall'n on evil days,
> On evil days though fall'n, and evil tongues;
> In darkness, and with dangers compast round,
> And solitude....

What strikes the modern student of the Romantics is not Milton's commonplace Renaissance request for a "fit audience, though few," but the rhetoric that emphasizes the poet's personal position, surrounded by dangers, alone with his half-finished epic and the company of the muse. While this alienation is seldom alluded to, it is in the background of Romantic fondness for the phrase, which takes on a new urgency as a result of a perceived fissure between the artist and his culture. But given the unprecedented popularity of long poems by Scott, Byron, Moore, and others, this desire for a small readership of hardy understanders seems rather curious; the aesthetics of difficulty, however, develop as a counter to an aesthetics of ease.

As early as 1800, Wordsworth complained of "the deluges of idle and extravagant stories in verse" and feared among readers a "degrading thirst after outrageous stimulation." The Gothic, in particular, dulled the imagination and kept readers from constructing a reading of a poem such as "Simon Lee." Walter Scott's popular poems provided another model that encouraged reading for pleasure only. In the preface to *The Bridal of Triermain* (1813), Scott argues that "Romantic Poetry . . . comprehends a fictitious narrative, framed and combined at the pleasure of the writer. . . . everything is permitted to him, excepting to be heavy or prosaic, for which, free and unembarrassed as he is, he has no manner of apology."[2] But this freedom is also a limitation, since it excludes the seriousness of purpose that marks the epic as the locus for the loftiest ambition of any young poet. While Scott's definition frees the poet from direct competition with the past — by excluding the epic tradition, the poet becomes "unembarrassed" — it seems to impose the necessity of being "light and poetic" for an entire book-length effort. The poems that result, as Hazlitt notes in his essay on Moore, go to extraordinary lengths to relieve the reader "from the fatigue of thought or shock of feeling."[3] But even Walter Scott could be too fatiguing for some critics. *The British Review* confesses itself unable to cope with the intricacies of *Rokeby*, and lays down a telling recipe for the long poem, worth quoting at length:

> We have no hesitation in stating it as our opinion, that a complicated tale is unfit for poetical effort, and that where the imagination is to be exalted, and the feelings excited, the mind ought not to be put upon any strong spontaneous effort. The happiest posture in which the mind of the reader can be for the purposes of the poet, is that docile resignation of feeling, which submits to be moved and directed whichever way the poet turns his magic sceptre. . . . But when we are involved in the entanglements of an intricate plot, we feel either in a state of actual embarrassment, or in a perpetual peril of losing ourselves, from which the effort to escape agitates and fatigues the mind, and creates a sort of friction that retards the wheels of the imagination.[4]

This is an extraordinary passage, because it clearly states the usually unstated, Johnsonian belief in the reader's right-to-understand. As we shall see, by the time of *Sordello* an exactly opposite view — that the text should agitate and exercise the reader to the point of fatigue — will be more frequently iterated.

By the 1820s, booksellers looked to find easy poems that would sell,

16

and poets and critics looked for difficult poems that would exercise their readers. Peacock's analysis of the situation in a letter to Shelley accurately captures a fear generated by the changes in the make-up of the reading public: "The truth," he says, "is that there is no longer a poetical audience among the higher class of minds. . . . the poetical reading public, being composed of the mere dregs of the intellectual community, the most sufficing passport to their favour must rest on the mixture of a little easily-intelligible portion of mawkish sentiment, with an absolute negation of reason and knowledge."[5] By the 1830s, what remained of the audience for poetry favored the sentimentality of "L.E.L." and the picture-book annuals, and many publishing houses refused to consider new poems at all. When a serious poem did break into print, the prognosis was not good. Henry Taylor published *Philip van Artevelde* in 1834, and Lockhart immediately predicted that the fluffy lyric that links the two parts of the lengthy epic/drama would be the most popular part of the poem. This song is introduced, satirically, by the following couplet:

> Turn thou the page, and let thy senses drink
> A lay that shall not trouble thee to think.[6]

By the 1830s, the unthinking "public" reader has become an object of ridicule, like Sterne's "Madam," to be pacified with a pretty lyric. But well before this time, an evolving notion of a "fit audience" has become the norm for the ambitious poet.

The progress of this attitude can be traced by following some of the uses of Milton's phrase from the first generation of Romantics through the third generation — poets such as Browning and Tennyson, who, accepting in their youth variations of the "fit audience" maxim, ironically lived on to enjoy notable popular acclaim. It is clear, I think, that the dogma of the fit audience contributes directly to canon formation, and to the increasing narrative disjunctiveness and stylistic complexity of texts in the first half of the century, because the rhetorical target has an inevitable impact on the text, and taking aim at a "fit" group of understanders must change poetic style. A self-conscious elite may place a maximum value on art that it feels is shunned by the masses, or is too sophisticated for the average reader, and the poet who would wish to address *only* this audience would insulate himself stylistically from popular culture, altering his methods to provide his clique with the pleasures they demand. Other writers, genuinely alienated, may choose to accept only a small audience, because they cannot honestly address the "public." Poets such as Wordsworth try to take a middle ground, directing their work towards a fit audience, but not for a coterie. As Wordsworth's fame begins to grow in the late-1820s and 1830s, his appreciators sound a common note: they are proud to be among the initial few, but eager to spread the word to all who will listen.

The audience becomes, because of its importance to the author's preferred strategy of dissemination, the key to its shape. A clear case of stylistic evolution to fit the audience can be discerned with Coleridge; in his later writings the desire to reach a specific audience of educated and conservative readers leads to the development of a difficult prose style, as well as the later sage-like personal presence. Marilyn Butler, in her recent survey of the background to English Romantic literature, argues that in these works Coleridge's "strangely specialized tone made a kind of compact with the reader, flatteringly promoting him to membership among the elect."[7] If the desire to avoid addressing "the people" (a sleeping dog better let lie) shapes Coleridge's Tory polemics, the desire to reach and rouse the people through the development of disciples whose enthusiasm would leapfrog the usual arbiters of "public" taste is the norm of the radical Shelley, who uses this argument to rationalize his esoteric mode in *Prometheus Unbound*. By the 1830s, from any political vista one chooses, critical opinion leans towards the denigration of works popular with either the people or the "public," and thus valorizes difficult, or at least unpopular, modes.

The desire for a select readership (without the feelings of alienation) is put forward by Dryden as well as Milton; in his dedication to the *Aeneis* (1697) he calls for a small class of readers who are "souls of the highest rank and truest understanding." These elect will then act as apostles for the poet, because of a "certain magnetism in their judgement, which then attracts others to their sense. Every day they gain some new proselyte, and in time become the Church."[8] An apostolic role for the reader appealed to the Romantics — both the poets and their small bands of reader-champions — who felt that the bard's prophetic message must be spread throughout the world in order to influence change. The paradigm of the Apostles also helped to align a disappointingly small audience with large ambitions, political as well as poetical. Leigh Hunt notes in 1810 that the taste of Italy "was created by a few great artists, and so it must be with other countries, just as poets and not critics create rules and taste for poetry."[9] Wordsworthians such as Crabb Robinson and De Quincey saw their poet through the filter of the fit audience paradigm, and in the "prospectus" which concludes his preface to *The Excursion*, Wordsworth, after a grand declaration of the subject of his song, quotes Milton:

> Of the individual Mind that Keeps her own
> Inviolate retirement, subject there
> To Conscience only, and the law supreme
> Of that Intelligence which governs all;
> I sing: — "fit audience let me find though few!"[10]

Wordsworth's *Excursion* lays the groundwork for the fame that would make him the most important poet of the 1830s, and this invocation of the fit audience refers not only to Milton's epic muse but also to the example of Milton's poetic career — a career, in the words of Walter Scott, in which the foundations of fame are laid "in silence and secrecy."[11] In order to verify the importance of the received picture of Milton's career to Wordsworth, we have only to look to the "Essay, Supplementary to the Preface" of 1815, in which Wordsworth provides a conspectus of English literary history in order to prove that the best poets have always gained only a limited audience upon their first appearance.

In the "Essay" Wordsworth demonstrates that practically no one is qualified to judge new poetry, and argues that "it ought to follow that partial notice only, or neglect, perhaps long continued, or attention wholly inadequate to their merits — must have been the fate of most works in the higher departments of poetry." This deductive reasoning is then supported inductively by a "hasty retrospect of the poetical literature of this Country." The further conclusion drawn from the survey is that "every Author, as far as he is great and at the same time *original*, has had the task of *creating* the taste by which he is to be enjoyed; so has it been, so will it continue to be."[12] This is Wordsworth's explanation of his failure at the bookstalls (and perhaps an indirect hit at Byron), but it is also a rationale for his refusal to write in popular modes. It is typical, though, that in his final paragraph his democratic leanings should creep in; he asks,

> Is it the result of the whole that, in the opinion of the Writer, the judgment of the People is not to be respected? The thought is most injurious. . . . The People have already been justified . . . when it was said, above, that, of *good* Poetry, the *individual*, as well as the species, *survives*. And how does it survive but through the People. (pp. 186-87)

19

Wordsworth's characterization of the "People" here is to some degree abstracted; the word itself, as opposed to "Public," carries democratic connotations, and Wordsworth closes his essay with the intimation that the "fit audience" will eventually educate the taste of the people and thus insure the survival of poetry in an ever-widening audience. (The "people" thus defined, as we shall see, gather around Sordello at a crucial moment in Browning's poem.) The "People" are an evolutionary continuum of the "few scattered hearers" of the poet in his initial season, spread through the ages. "The Poet," to quote from the Preface of 1802, "binds together by passion and knowledge the vast empire of human society, as it spreads over the whole earth, and over all time" (p. 52).

Wordsworth's collection of 1815 contains a more or less complete literary theory embedded in the "Preface," "Preface to the Lyrical Ballads," and the "Essay," and the composite document, along with Wordsworth's poems about the poetic vocation, has an incalculable influence on the next two or three generations of poets. While much has been said of the theory of diction, and Coleridge's quarrel with it, the final word in the volume is Wordsworth's argument against popular poetry, and his endorsement of the practice of writing (especially the long poem) without a large readership in mind. This position is strengthened by Coleridge's application of Milton's phrase to Wordsworth's work in the *Biographia*:

> If Mr. Wordsworth is not equally with Daniel alike intelligible to all readers of average understanding in all passages of his works, the comparative difficulty does not arise from the greater impurity of the ore but from the nature and use of the metal. A poem is not necessarily obscure because it does not aim to be popular. It is enough if a work be perspicuous to those for whom it is written, and
> Fit audience find, though few.[13]

Wordsworth's proofs that quality and public acclaim do not go together are reiterated in many texts of the next thirty years, and this view is widely remarked upon within the context of the "Laker School" of poetry. In the eyes of the press, members of this "school" accept the premises of Wordsworth's prefaces and write to the "fit audience" with a surety of posthumous renown. In the *Noctes Ambrosianae*, for instance, when North questions the Ettrick Shepherd about the success of his epic *Queen Hynde* (1825), the following exchange occurs:

20

Shepherd.   Success! She's no had muckle o' that, man. Me and Wordsworth are aboon the age we live in — it's no worthy o' us; but wait a whylock — wait only a thousand years, or thereabouts, Mr. North, and you'll see who will have speeled to the tap o' the tree.

North.   Nay, James, you are by far too popular at present to be entitled to posthumous fame.[14]

While *Blackwood's* is ever joking, this reflects the feeling of the times, and Wilson, who had begun his literary career as a quasi-Laker, was in a position to accurately satirize Wordsworth's view. Especially outside the lyric, late-Romantic and early-Victorian writers assume that a poet who aims for the summit must leave all but a perspicuous few behind on the lower slopes.

Of the younger Romantics, Shelley most frequently iterates the fit audience paradigm, though with significant variations, because he was never reconciled to the loss of "Public" acclaim, and vacillated in his aims towards the audience, on the one hand writing works which were studiously more esoteric than any attempted by Wordsworth, and on the other not merely striving for a Public success (as with *The Cenci*), but attempting to address poems and pamphlets to the widest and least discriminating audience, the "people" in the unWordsworthian sense of the democratic mob. His practice turned towards preparing each of his texts with a particular audience in mind — the instructions to the publisher Ollier clearly reveal this method: "*Prometheus Unbound*, I must tell you, is my favorite poem; I charge you, therefore, specially to pet him and feed him with fine ink and good paper. *Cenci* is written for the multitude, and ought to sell well. I think, if I may judge by its merits, the *Prometheus* cannot sell twenty copies."[15] Shelley implies that the poem's merits are sufficiently high to preclude popularity. Edward Williams, Shelley's friend, also thought of popularity and merit in inverse proportion. After Byron had shown him a book which violently abused his poetry, Williams wrote in his journal: "Such is ever the reward of exalted geniuses, and an author in the present times may almost be valued in proportion as the abuse of the world increases. S. and L.B. afford proofs among those who are living."[16]

Shelley was sensitive to this abuse, and when he planned publication of his *Epipsychidion* he directed Ollier to make a printing of only one hundred copies, because the poem was meant for the "esoteric few" and because "those who are capable of judging and feeling rightly with respect to a composition of so abstruse a nature, certainly do not arrive

21

at that number — among those at least, who would ever be excited to read an obscure and anonymous production; and it would give me no pleasure that the vulgar should read it."[17] (Browning's first poem, *Pauline*, was brought forth in just such a manner.) Shelley consciously placed *Epipsychidion* in a tradition of private poems by affixing a prefatory stanza from Dante's *Convivio* — the last stanza of the first canzone, which opens in Shelley's translation with an echo of Milton's "fit audience find, though few":

> My Song, I fear that thou wilt find but few
> Who fitly shall conceive thy reasoning,
> Of such hard matter dost thou entertain[.][18]

The hard matter of such a poem functions as a barrier to the uninitiated and makes the poem into a kind of test for the readers. Dante's poetry, which achieved a place as an acceptable model only in the early years of the nineteenth century, was considered by Shelley's contemporaries to be difficult; as Hazlitt put it, Dante is the poet "who relies most on . . . the sense of power in the reader — who leaves most to the imagination."[19]

But Shelley saw the role of the poet as twofold. In the first, more typically "Romantic," way, the poet writes for a select audience, and in the role of unacknowledged legislator eventually contributes to the amelioration of mankind's condition — the gospel slowly filters from poet, to reader-disciple, to the people. The second way, I think, is not as an unacknowledged legislator, but as a recognized and potent foe of unreformed legislatures, writing pieces such as "Song: Men of England." In his espousal of this double path, Shelley is unique among Romantic poets (if we may except Wordsworth's *Cintra* and other minor prose participations in current debates). His understanding of the poet's need for both a "fit audience, though few" and a voice in more raucous political dialogues of the day is instrumental in shaping the critical issues of the politically (and poetically) turbulent 1830s. But Shelley's attempt to reach Cobbett's audience directly through popular political rhymes was not pursued by any other major poets, for fear of stirring up the mob. Instead — as in *Sordello* — the issue becomes whether the poet should stick to the "fit audience" paradigm, or give up poetic power (as Byron seemed to do) for direct political action. Browning contemplates various careers, Tennyson makes an abortive attempt at succoring Spain, and Carlyle throughout the 1830s urges poets to give up poetry. In the meantime, the image of Shelley develops around his esoteric verse; Leigh Hunt in 1828 eulogizes Shelley in terms that would remain standard for the rest of the century (though Arnold and other Victorians would also use the same terms derogatorily):

> Mr. Shelley was in his whole being, mental and physical, of an extreme delicacy and sensibility. He felt every part of his nature intensely; and his impulse, object, and use in this world, was to remind others of some important points touching our common nature and endeavors.... Mr. Shelley's writings, it is admitted, are not calculated to be popular, however popular in their ultimate tendency, or cordial in their origin. They are, for the most part, too abstracted and refined. But "fit audience though few," is the motto of the noblest ambition; and it is these audiences that go and settle the world. [20]

Mary Shelley, when she finally received permission to collect Shelley's poems from her husband's family, introduces her edition of 1839 with the claim that Shelley has fulfilled the paradigm: "He died, and the world showed no outward sign. But his influence over mankind, though slow in growth, is fast augmenting; and, in the ameliorations that have taken place in the political state of his country, we may trace in part the operation of his arduous struggles." [21] And Mary was reiterating what had become common: Shelley, writes one critic in 1836, "can only affect the disposition of a few speculative and imaginative readers," but his influence, while "slow in its origin, and more limited in its circle [than Byron's]... continues, and will long continue to operate." [22]

Admirers of Shelley, it follows, would plan their own careers to follow a similar pattern. The writers of the 1830s accept "fit audience, though few" as their creed, and even extend it into unlikely places. Carlyle defends Burns (whose popular success was never in doubt) in an 1828 article in the *Edinburgh Review* by placing him in Milton's position: "not only low, but fallen from a height; not only poor, but impoverished; in darkness and in dangers compassed round, he sang his immortal song, and found fit audience, though few" (*Works*, 26, p. 312). Carlyle in fact constantly reiterates variations of the fit audience paradigm, and it especially presides over the composition of *The French Revolution*. He writes of this book that "there will [be] ten enemies of it for one friend; but also that it will find friends by and by"; and in a letter to Emerson he shows his contempt for the Public: "Beat this thing, I say always, under thy dull hoofs, O dull Public, trample it and tumble it into all sinks and kennels; if thou canst kill it, kill it in God's name: if thou canst not kill it, why then thou wilt not." To his brother John, Carlyle states clearly the powers of the initial few: "small praise will it look for; at best, much censure," but the few who appreciate *The French Revolution* will constitute "real *votes*, and outweigh all the babble or no-babble that is, was or will be." This attitude, Carlyle realizes, affects his style; later in 1835 he again writes John that "it will be a queer Book; one of the *queerest* published in this Century, and *can*, though it cannot be popular, be better than that."[23] Browning's *Sordello*, as we shall see, represents a culmination of sorts of the troping of style to represent the necessity of fitting the audience to the poem — the reciprocity between intended reader and poetic form is one of its themes.

This contempt for the public is present in many writers of the 1830s. In 1831, when Arthur Hallam publishes his review of Tennyson's *Poems, Chiefly Lyrical*, he explicitly follows Wordsworth by opening with a furious attack on "that hydra, the Reading Public." He notes approvingly that Tennyson is a "young poet . . . not studious of instant popularity, and not likely to obtain it," and concludes with a somewhat jejune disdain for contemporary readers: "We have spoken in good faith, commending this volume to feeling hearts and imaginative tempers, not to the stupid readers, or the voracious readers, or the malignant readers, or the readers after dinner!"[24] In Browning's *Paracelsus* the learned doctor, who is presented as a type of poet / creative genius, learns the fickleness of the Public, and tells Festus that after the major portion of the audience is discounted:

> remains
> A scantling — a poor dozen at the best —
> Worthy to look for sympathy and service,
> And likely to draw profit from my pains.   (III, 634-37)

Browning's scantling — an apostolic dozen — go out, one presumes, and settle the world. As the reviewer in *The Metropolitan Magazine* (October, 1835) concluded, *Paracelsus* "is a poem ambitiously unpopular" (*Correspondence*, 3, p. 352), and Browning (while happy) must have been surprised and even a bit abashed by its relative popularity. His next poem, too, is ambitious in its address to the fit audience, with more predictable success (or failure). Notice in the periodical Reviews is good, providing it is bad; "God send I be not too proud of their abuse!" writes Browning, "For there is no hiding the fact that it is of the proper old drivelling virulence with which God's Elect have in all ages been regaled" (*RB & AD*, p. 56).

The notion of the fit audience, coupled with the notion that poetic laurels are signaled by abusive criticism, contributes strongly to canon formation, too. The collapse of Byron's reputation after 1825 among the "fit audiences" such as the Cambridge "Apostles" was caused partly by the damning evidence of his enormous sales; there was a converse attraction in championing Keats and Shelley when they were unknown or infamous. Browning's boyhood espousal of Shelley is well-known; Shelley replaced Byron in his estimation, and Browning valued Shelley all the more because in the 1820s his work had to be obtained in a semiconspiratorial manner.[25] One of the curious principles of canon formation at this time, in fact, is a tendency to value writers in proportion to the amount of abuse they receive, and to exclude writers (such as Lockhart) who participate in the attacks. Carlyle proudly reprinted bad criticism in the second edition of *The French Revolution*, knowing that this would serve to advertise the work's merits among the "fit audience" better than would periodical praise. One passage (from Horne's and Elizabeth Barrett's essay on Tennyson in *A New Spirit of the Age*) may serve as a summary example; in an account of the "misprision" of Tennyson's public reception they conclude:

> While the 'Byron School' was in its glory, it is no great wonder that Wordsworth should have been a constant laughing-stock, and Keats an object for contemptuous dismissal to the tomb. It must, however, be added that the marked neglect of the public towards the latter has continued down to the present day.... But if there be faith in the pure Ideal, and in the progress of intelligence and refinement, the ultimate recognition of Keats by the public will certainly follow that of the 'fit audience' which he will ever continue to possess. Of all the numerous imitators of Lord Byron, not one now remains. And this may be mentioned as a quiet commentary upon his supercilious fling at the superior genius of John Keats.[26]

The paradigm of the fit audience demonstrated in this passage is thoroughly commonplace by 1844, when Keats was widely recognized as a great poet unfairly abused. Writers such as Horne, in fact, often seem to imagine that the abuse continues, when in fact it does not.

There is a strong connection between the acceptance of the fit audience paradigm, the consideration of abuse as proof of quality, and the aesthetics of difficulty. The ramifications of the fit audience doctrine, along with the general feeling that the new steam-intellect age was unsuitable for poetry, materially affect the genre of the long poem. In Heraud's "Cambrian Colloquy," the "major" presents an organic view of poetry, derived from Coleridge, but an apt image for poems written to a "fit audience"; he comments on the decline in the fortune of poetry from Byron's day:

> this constrained obliquity in development in poor poetry (left in the dark to shoot how it can, like a weed, instead of being cherished like a glorious flower, as it always has been), reminds me of a phenomenon in plants, whose instinctive seeming effort to reach the sun's influence is like that of your poet to get a bask in the sunshine of fame. If you place a plant in a flower-pot in a dark room, with but *one hole admitting light*, you shall see it contorting its shoots, and pointing them in a surprising manner to attain that hole, which having passed through, up they spring again, and no more creep and writhe, but flourish upright in the sun's eye, which they had languished for.[27]

Heraud's image plausibly anticipates (and explains) the style of *Sordello*, in which Browning's rhymes, in his own words, "spring, dispread, / Dispart, disperse" until they achieve the light and become "thick foliaged next, a-shiver soon / With coloured buds" (II, 593-99). But in order to reach the one hole of light — the few readers — the poet requires co-operation; long poems, as they become more complex and difficult, move towards greater reader participation. In the old dichotomy of beautiful and sublime, the former is scorned as too easy, and the sublime is transmogrified; the idea of what is beautiful in poetry (and thus what is poetic) moves from the pretty expression of feeling and sentiment to the difficult poetic compression of feeling and thought — to be fully shared, not merely listened to or appreciated. The way in which writers recognized the need for greater reader response in their works, is the subject of the next section.

II

"The reader indeed — that great idea!" —DE QUINCEY

De Quincey follows this exclamation with the statement that the reader "is often a more important person towards the fortune of an essay than the writer."[28] Although he is ostensibly beginning an essay on Milton (in *Blackwood's*, 1839), De Quincey goes on to propose several images for "those well-known parties to a book — writer and reader." One view is of the writer, full of authority, speaking *ex cathedra*, who "conceits himself booted and spurred, and mounted on his reader's back, with an express commission for riding him." But De Quincey leans towards an opposite view, in which "the reader is sovereign" (pp. 396-97); unfortunately his interesting digression, as so often, is cut short by the commencement of

26

his stated subject. Romantic writers, in their various roles as critics, poets, diarists, and correspondents, draw from the experience of reading and from their sense of what a fit audience might be to define a role for the reader that increasingly tends to valorize an active relationship between writer, reader, and literary work. Surveying the range of Romantic statements about creative reading, we find that these statements prepare the ground for an aesthetic of difficulty that finds its zenith in the early works of Carlyle and Browning.

De Quincey's two models of reading may be taken as emblems for the reader's role. The first view, in which the writer masters the reader, is one in which the reader is passively enthralled. In the words of the *British Review* essay on Walter Scott (previously quoted), the reader with "docile resignation . . . submits to be moved and directed whichever way the poet turns his magic sceptre." This enchantment of reading appeals to naive readers (including children who, like Wordsworth and Coleridge as boys, were devoted to the Arabian Nights), and those who tend to see reading primarily as a pleasurable intermingling of minds. The work of Georges Poulet provides a modern parallel; for Poulet, reading is a unique activity which attenuates the usual distance between subject and object, and allows the reader to be the subject of another's thoughts; in order for this to happen, the reader must surrender:

> When I read as I ought, i.e. without mental reservation, without any desire to preserve my independence of judgement, and with the total commitment required of any reader, my comprehension becomes intuitive and any feeling proposed to me is immediately assumed by me.[29]

For Poulet, the criticism of identification (or intersubjectivity) is a Romantic invention which he traces back to Mme de Staël's early work on Rousseau, where she declares "le *souvenir* et l'impression de mon *enthousiasme*" — a remembered identification in which the critic revives and shares the genius of the creator.[30] Poulet's reader is essentially happy, an Epicurean of intersubjectivity. The Romantics who most resemble him are Charles Lamb and Leigh Hunt, who are able to appreciate a wide variety of texts through a protean ability to become at will what the work requires. Hunt always views his readers as friends, and believes we should read "to have human nature reflected" on us, not to impose on the book our own unchanging prejudices.[31] The reader's imagination is thus not radically creative but mimetic, and indicative of a certain free range of sympathy.

Reading "without mental reservation," however attractive from one standpoint, has its limitations; the rhetoric of enthrallment has all too obvious connections to the politics of tyranny — to the notion that any other kind of response except enthrallment is inappropriate. There is also the fear that the too-dominant writer will exert a bad moral effect on the too-submissive reader. Early nineteenth-century writers kept in mind the infamous case of a German nobleman supposed to have taken up the career of Schiller's "Robber" — it reminded them of the dangers of literature for the impressionable mind. Later, the quick sway of Byron's poetry over the popular imagination led to criticism, in John Wilson's phrase, that he "aims in poetry, like the fallen chief whose image is so often before him [Napoleon], at universal dominion, we had almost said, universal tyranny, over the minds of men."[32] There is, too, something sinister in the conservative Southey's declaration that "it is a great thing to write for readers who are disposed to assent to everything you say."[33] Coleridge, more evasive, added an Estecean preface to his "Fire, Famine, and Slaughter" when he reprinted it in *Sibylline Leaves* (1817) to prove that it could not corrupt common readers: "the poem was not calculated to excite passion in any mind, or to make any impression except on *poetic* readers."[34] De Quincey's image of the "booted and spurred" writer reflects fears of the power of writing, and denounces implicitly all overbearing and dogmatic texts which, in their overdeterminations, leave no room for the exercise of the reader's imagination.

From the other side, some of the clearest invitations to the reader to join in the production of the text, as is well known, can be found in popular eighteenth-century fiction (and in the seed-text of the novel, *Don Quixote*). In these books the reader is signaled or directed clearly at the place in which he is to take an active part — the writer, like the orchestra conductor — waves the baton towards the person in the armchair. In *Joseph Andrews*, for instance, Fielding's playful personification of the morning — "That beautiful young lady the Morning now rose from her bed" — is closed by a simile: "like Miss ———,*" with a footnote that reads, "*Whoever the reader pleases."[35] Fielding implies that however skillful his description is, the (presumably male) reader's imagination will complete the picture with his own amorous ideal. In *Tristram Shandy*, Sterne trumps Fielding by introducing not a blank for a name, but an entire page for the reader's erotic description, ordering him to "Sit down, Sir, paint her to your own mind — as like your mistress as you can ... please but your own fancy in it."[36] For Sterne, as for De Quincey, writer and reader are co-equal parties to the text: "The

Truest respect which you can pay to your reader's understanding is to halve the matter amicably, and leave him something to imagine, in his own turn as well as yourself. For my own part I am eternally paying him compliments of this kind, and do all in my power to keep his imagination as busy as my own" (p. 83). While Romantic poems are not versified *Shandys*, Sterne's novel exists for subsequent writers as a chirographic license for a rhetoric structured around the concept of the reader's supplying textual chasms. Wordsworth's temperament is almost the exact opposite of Sterne's, yet in a letter of 1791 he confesses ignorance of modern literature, "excepting in our own language three volumes of *Tristram Shandy*."[37] Southey proposes to emulate the novelist more directly, planning a work in 1805 that "should have all that is odd and grotesque in sublimity, puns by the wholesale — chapters of rhymes and plenty of the unintelligible with a few stars * * * * * to enlighten it, out Rabelaising Rabelais out Sternifying Sterne."[38] And Browning signals his connection to this tradition of the novel by his opening allusion to *Don Quixote* in *Sordello*, though his invitations to fill in the gaps are never as overt or specific as those in eighteenth-century fiction.

If Sterne was the most famous example for the Romantics, there were other, more sober, theorists who sought to focus attention on reader participation. Archibald Alison notes how, when the reader is involved in the train of associations produced by the text, "the object itself appears only to serve as a hint to awaken the imagination, and to lead it through every analogous idea. . . . It is then, indeed, in this powerless state of revery, when we are carried on by our conceptions, not guiding them, that the deepest emotions of beauty or sublimity are felt."[39] Alison here has transferred, without comment, the rapture of the poet to the reader; association theory, with its emphasis in Sterne and Alison on reader psychology, shifts the balance from the poet's experience in making the text to the reader's feelings while re-making it. In a poem which may owe something to a reading of Alison, Wordsworth provides in "Simon Lee" a clear statement of the need for reader response. Geoffrey Hartman notes that Wordsworth's authorial intrusiveness in this poem follows Sterne more closely than any poetic predecessor, but it is not the direct address to the reader so much as what the reader is urged to do that is of interest:

> My gentle Reader, I perceive
> How patiently you've waited,
> And now I fear that you expect
> Some tale will be related.

O Reader! had you in your mind
Such stores as silent thought can bring,
O gentle Reader! you would find
A tale in every thing.
What more I have to say is short,
And you must kindly take it:
It is not a tale; but should you think,
Perhaps a tale you'll make it.[40]

"Simon Lee" instructs us how to read; a poem activates reader-thought, which generates a "tale" in the slightest of incidents; or, the feeling is the poet's, and the narrative is the sequence of effects upon the reader.

Renewed interest in the concept of active reading cannot be separated from other trends; there are so many overt statements of the necessity of reader response because for perhaps the first time a number of genres were popular which required minimal reader activity; true "light literature" is a product of the increase of literacy in industrial societies. The effect of the widespread acceptance of the "fit audience" paradigm reverberates through generic norms, changing and mutating them. Readers begin to define the generic differences in prose and verse narrative according to the degree of exertion required on their part. Long poems, considered as the most sublime genre, were thus inevitably difficult and demanded more perspicuous readers. Coleridge admits that a long poem cannot be "all poetry" (or lyric gusts), but he argues that all parts should excite "a more continuous and equal attention" than prose.[41] Poems that seemed easy were suspected by the fit and few. Crabb Robinson zipped through Southey's *Madoc* (1805), noting that it "has all the interest of a Novel"; he goes on, however, to say that "this ought not to be the feeling in reading poetry, which ought to require effort in the perusal."[42] Most readers of long poems felt that, if the poem aimed for the highest mark, reading it should be a bit of an ordeal. During these years even poems by culturally conservative writers have experimental and at least superficially difficult forms.

To cite one unheralded example, Samuel Rogers published in 1812 a poem about the discoverer of the New World. "The Voyage of Columbus" is a fictional edition which purports to be a fragmentary epic penned by a shipmate of the hero and just now translated; it is thus, in the words of Rogers' preface, "sudden in its transitions, and full of historical allusions; leaving much to the imagination of the reader."[43] The peculiar character of the poem he ascribes to the "old Spanish Chroniclers of the sixteenth century" whose "narratives are so many moving pictures of the actions, manners, and thoughts of their contemporaries" (p. 223). The astute "editor" proves in his notes that the poem, because of certain anachronisms, must have been written by someone in the next generation after Columbus. The text is framed by an "Inscription" spoken by the manuscript *in propria scriptura*, and concludes with a coda of "romance" stanzas "in another hand" (p. 226) which we are to believe tell the story of a meeting of Pizarro and Cortez in the church where Columbus first makes his entry into Spain. Rogers' structure, in short, is not unworthy of one of Borges' bookish "fictions," though the labyrinthean manifestations of the text seem more complex in the retelling than they are in the original.

What ties many of the long poems together, by both major and minor authors, is thus their difficulty and the extent to which they openly enlist reader participation. Inability to comprehend a single word of a new poem becomes, according to Peacock, a "standard joke" in the reviews, and Coleridge moans that perplexed readers account for their own "lack of intellect" by "declaring the author unintelligible."[44] As the century goes on, the reader is challenged both more seriously and more obliquely. Hallam notes that since the "demand on the reader for activity ... is the very same thing that moves his bile, it is obvious that those writers will be the most popular who require the least degree of exertion."[45] The implied correlative is that all great poets require the highest level of activity; we can note the change in the reputation of Scott, who, as we have seen, was chastized in the first years of the century for asking too much of his readers. In 1838, when Carlyle ruminates on Scott at the request of J. S. Mill, he dismisses Scott's poems because they invite the reader to relax:

> The reader, what the vast majority of readers so long to do, was allowed to lie down at his ease, and be ministered to. What the Turkish bathkeeper is said to aim at with his frictions, and shampooings, and fomentings, more or less effectually, that the patient in total idleness may have the delights of activity, —was here to a considerable degree realized.   (*Works*, 29, p. 57)

But if the reader is denied his Turkish Bath, in what manner must he exercise himself?

Carlyle provides the answer to this question, one provoked by his scoffing at his countryman's page-turning readability: the reader must put his shoulder to the work of the book, because not to do so is intellectual sloth. Coleridge earlier declares: "A lazy half-attention amounts to a mental yawn. ... we must be willing to exert a portion of

31

the...effort, and to think with the author, or the author will have thought in vain for us."[46] Carlyle's definite ideas about reading can be summarized in one word: *toil*. The reader who struggles is the reader who becomes a friend; the camaraderie of reader and writer is a sweaty bond of co-workers. Readers of this sort, few in number, become brother authors, or readerly kin to the writer. Carlyle's "fit audience" ideal governed the two harrowing years he spent writing (and rewriting) *The French Revolution*, and he refused to change his overly figural style to cater to popular taste. The last page contains a telling apostrophe to the reader on the necessity of "hearing truly":

> And so here, O Reader, has the time come for us two to part. *Toilsome* was our journeying together; not without offence; but it is done. To me thou wert as a beloved shade, the disembodied or not yet embodied spirit of a Brother. To thee I was but as a Voice. Yet was our relation a kind of sacred one; doubt not that! For whatsoever once sacred things become hollow jargons, yet while the Voice of Man speaks with Man, hast thou not there the living fountain out of which all sacrednesses sprang, and will yet spring? Man, by the nature of him, is definable as 'an incarnated Word.' Ill stands it with me if I have spoken falsely: thine also it was to hear truly. Farewell.
>
> (*Works*, 4, p. 323)

Carlyle's rhetorical embrace of the reader is not an anomaly. Despite vigorous expression of contempt for the "Public," the reigning image of the reader among Romantic writers is always the "friend": in Wordsworth's simple declaration, the poet is a man speaking to men. In Carlyle, the voice meets the brother spirit, and from the living fountain springs "all sacrednesses" — and the complete (because confluent) work of art. Carlyle's combination of both Romantic sublime and, especially in *Sartor*, the play of Romantic irony (developed from both Sterne and his own much-admired Teutons), makes him a kindred spirit to poets from Wordsworth to Browning. As Mill recognized (though prompted by Carlyle himself) in the first sentence of his review of *The French Revolution*: "This is not so much a history, as an epic poem."[47]

Carlyle's reader is both the passive reader who surrenders to the text (under the sway of "a Voice") and embodies in his own consciousness the spirit of the brother, and the active reader (Carlyle's "incarnated Word") who picks up the conversation and co-structures textual meaning. A good example occurs in *Sartor Resartus*: the editor selects from a paper-bag a "Moral relation" but the "reader for himself weaving it in at the right place" will then conclude "the arras-picture of these university years" (1:93). While the active and passive positions seem opposite, they are both based on a principle of intersubjectivity; it is this fraternal notion of the reader's relation to the writer which is shared by most Romantic writers.

Carlyle is also aware of another possibility, that there will arise assiduous tillers of the text who, like Byron's Cain, "never could / Reconcile what I saw with what I heard."[48] In the fissures of the text these readers may establish a position antithetical to the writer's; in *Sartor*, the editor exists as a mediator precisely because the English Public cannot be left to their own devices with the Clothes Philosophy. Other misreadings may become willful challenges to the authority of writers. Poetry may be admired at the wrong place, for the wrong reasons, but Shelley's and Blake's readings of Milton, to cite two famous examples, are something more than this. Blake's unfinished poem "The Everlasting Gospel" directly confronts the problem of rebellious reading, and *joys* in it: "Both read the Bible day & night / But thou readst black where I read white."[49] Counter readings during this period can serve political purposes, or act as testing grounds for the originality of the critic. Gabriele Rossetti's *Analytic Commentary on the Divine Comedy* (1826) is a famous attempt to prove that Dante was an anti-papal Freemason; it is easy to write this off as wrongheaded scholarship, but we may also consider it an inspired reading in Blake's sense, a substituting of white for black. Readings such as Rossetti's showed for Browning's age the extent to which literary texts are open, or ready for conquest; we need to understand how writers such as Carlyle and Browning, while accepting the potential reversal of figures implied in the aesthetics of difficulty, attempt to structure the reader's response through textual devices that order the reader's creativity or free play of thought to prevent the text from becoming radically indeterminate, while at the same time appealling to the readers' pleasure in the exercise of their own creative imaginations.

Browning's *Sordello*, like other works in the same mode, aspires in part to be a harsh taskmaster. These works can give, as Carlyle recognizes, and is too proud of giving, "offence"; not the least of the difficult poem's transgressions is the exuberance of its violation of generic borders. Readerly texts can give way to writerly texts with such glee that they become hieroglyphs with no critical Rosetta stone, something Browning's works were often accused of being late in the century, but were not. *Sui generis* becomes the refrain. One of Friedrich Schlegel's aphorisms states that "the modern poetic types are either only one or infinite in number. Each poem is a genre in itself."[50] Schlegel's comments "On Popular Poetry," excerpted in the *New Monthly* (1830) in the "Specimens of German Genius," is instructive; he contrasts the eighteenth-century view of Burger that poetry to be perfect must be popular with the Romantic ideal of unpopularity, and, like Wordsworth, finds that poetic history bears out his findings: "Dante and Petrarch, the two great fathers of modern poetry, are, in every sense of the word . . . as unpopular as it is possible to be." Clarity is not necessarily an end in itself, for in some poems "a veil of intricacy and obscurity contributes to make the desired impression."[51] The incomprehensible in poetry, then, becomes a generic trait that escapes the traditional taxonomy of genres; the more closely a poem adheres to generic norms, the harder it is to make it difficult. Schlegel's argument concludes, again like Wordsworth's, with the idea that true "popular poetry" — the mysterious poetry of the Bible, or Shakespeare's tragedies — lasts because the proper effect of poetry on the reader is the stimulation of the imagination, not the immediate and clear apprehension of determinate meaning. This poetic is widespread in the 1830s, and frequently spoofed in such journals as *Blackwood's*, *Fraser's*, and *Tait's*. The review of *Paracelsus* in *Leigh Hunt's London Journal* perfectly sums this poetic up:

> There is much both in the diction and the versification which has a harsh, awkward, and disappointing affect at first; but this, in by far the greater part, arises merely from the poem not being cast in a common mould, or formed so much as most new poems are upon the ordinary models. It is not a mere additional variation of the old air; and it cannot therefore be read off-hand so readily and smoothly as the generality of the poetical productions of the day. . . . The reader of such a work has his effort to make, as well as the writer has had his — his powers of apprehension, as the other has had his powers of production, to keep on the stretch.   (*Correspondence*, 3, p. 358)

Browning's next poem continues to stretch generic boundaries and stylistic norms.

While the variations in Romantic texts are seemingly endless — in Tieck's "Puss in Boots" the audience argues about the play and the players complain about their parts — and the generic frontiers are sometimes more fascinating than the lands they ring, it is also true that the difficult Romantic text can be seen as conforming to one type: texts that make singular requests (demands) to the reader to exercise creativity. Many names have been suggested for the metamorphic romantic text — many of them found in the subtitles to books from the 1790s through the

1830s. The structuring of the text so that the reader is compelled to fill in and not merely leap over (in the time-honored way of under-reading), is what is important, not the already questionable generic distinctions. In *Sordello*, a "load every rift with ore" aesthetic works alongside a deliberately wayward excavation of abysses for the reader to bridge (or fall into). This strategy has yet to be named. While this is no place for an exhaustive survey of modern reader response theory, the work of Wolfgang Iser may help us to situate a general act of reading against the particular experience of reading *Sordello*.

III

Most theorists of reader response would agree that the "work" emerges through the interaction of the reader with the text, existing only in a limbo between the two; the work, Iser states "must inevitably be virtual in character, as it cannot be reduced to the reality of the text or to the subjectivity of the reader."[52] Iser's analysis of exactly how the reader "performs" depends heavily on the notion of "gaps," "blanks," and "spots of indeterminacy" that he owes to the work of Roman Ingarden, though Iser places more emphasis on the reader's role, and eschews any concept of optimal readers and bad readers. But it is the concept of "gaps" that provides a strong link between a Romantic aesthetics of difficulty and modern phenomenological theory.

The "blanks" in the text are the pivotal spots in the system of the text which must be reconstituted through another system, that of the reader; "the structured blanks of the text," according to Iser, "stimulate the process of ideation to be performed by the reader on terms set by the text" (*Act of Reading*, p. 169). In this act, the "theme and horizon" continually switch back and forth in the time-flow of the act of reading and enable meaning to be realized. This too is also an attribute of the text, and enables the reader to "gradually take over the author's unfamiliar view of the world on the terms laid down by the author" (*Act of Reading*, p. 97). Iser thus provides a theory that takes into account the conditioned indeterminacy of textual schemata that invoke the reader's own capabilities and creativity without allowing for complete freedom; the text (and the author) "prefigure what the reader is given to ideate."[53] The relevance of Iser's position becomes clear, I think, when we consider that many Romantic writers, including the young Robert Browning, are allured by the notion of free-floating signifiers, but they too pull back from the brink of radical indeterminacy.

Iser has been attacked on a number of counts, most heavily on his perception of literature's uniqueness (it is easy enough to see that all discourse is full of "blanks"). Stanley Fish finds that Iser's theory falls apart over the question of the determinate nature of the text. He states in a *Diacritics* review that "in his more characteristic moments Iser insists on the brute-fact status of the text, at least insofar as it provides directions for the assembling of the 'virtual object.'" And Fish convincingly destroys Iser's differentiation between literature and quotidian speech-acts, showing that they are both essentially indeterminate.[54] But Iser is also criticized by Dagmar Barnouw for an exactly opposite reason; Barnouw charges that Iser causes the text to disappear, that its status isn't "brute-fact" at all. What is more interesting, he contends that Iser values gap-filled(?) texts over determinate ones, and thus excludes certain kinds of texts (and readings) from the canon. Barnouw goes on to assert that Iser neglects the idea that "indeterminacy (*Unbestimmtheit*) is a conscious strategy of the author and as such [is] in need of interpretation."[55]

Browning, I believe, develops just such a strategy through his reading of Romantic texts and Romantic poetics. The terms of the debate would have been familiar to Romantic writers; for them the ordinary versus poetic language dispute had become a matter of jest. In the "Noctes Ambrosianae," for instance, Tickler declares that "poets are a set of very absurd inhabitants of this earth. The simple fact of their presuming to have a language of their own should have dished them centuries ago."[56] Iser's notions of "gaps" that are stored and filled as the reader goes along, and his insistence that the reader's imaginative creation of the work effects a change upon the consciousness of the reader, can be assimilated easily to a Romantic rhetoric of poetry, and used to explain how some difficult and experimental texts function. Iser's gaps lead the reader to an experience of defamiliarization, and this shift in the reader's perspective, in which old habits of thought seem novel, leads Iser into the hoary moral argument that literature broadens our horizons: "The efficacy of a literary text is brought about by the apparent evocation and subsequent negation of the familiar. . . . it is only when we have outstripped our preconceptions and left the shelter of the familiar that we are in a position to gather new experiences."[57] For Romantic poets, reorientation (which a late-eighteenth-century critic such as Archibald Alison termed the effect of the sublime) is part of the repertory of genres such as the epic, "lyrical ballad," and grand ode.

While Iser's theory is essentially ahistorical, he notes in passing that literature since the eighteenth century has become increasingly indeterminate, requiring "correspondingly greater demands on the reader's structuring activity" (*Act of Reading*, p. 205). Since the days of Sterne the number and kinds of books that depend on the reader's imaginative participation has increased, and this coincides with a marked change in size and cultural level in the reading public. The recital of complaints against lazy reading, the pride in abuse by "Public" critics, and the cultivation of novel genres, form part of Romanticism's reaction to changed conditions for authorship. The intersection of the fit audience paradigm with the concerns of both liberal and conservative Romantic writers about the reading public engenders the production of works, like *Sordello*, that seem designed to prove the concept that the reader half-creates the work being read.

While Iser draws heavily on a narrow range of examples — mostly canonical novels from Fielding to Joyce — it is clear that the long poem during the same period also develops around the reader. Indeed, we would be hard put to find a better record of reader-response than Coleridge's account of hearing his friend recite the *Prelude*:

> My soul lay passive, by thy various strain
> Driven as in surges now beneath the stars,
> With momentary stars of my own birth,
> Fair constellated foam, still darting off
> Into the darkness; now a tranquil sea,
> Outspread and bright, yet swelling to the moon.[58]

Coleridge's "momentary stars" record the process of "reading" the *Prelude*, constellating for the moment one meaning, modifying it in the next as the poem progresses. But Coleridge also produces his own work, "constellated" or under the influence of the work read; the final image is of the soul impregnated, "outspread and bright, yet swelling to the moon." While Coleridge's imagery reveals much about his own psychology and dependence on Wordsworth, it also reflects his belief that the great long poem, more than any other work, should leave the reader swollen with his own poetry, even if this "poetry" is, in form, only an interpretation, or a record of a particular reading experience.

Iser uses the analogy of the constellation, too; it is the key to his explanation of how individual readings vary, yet may not be totally random:

> In the same way, two people gazing at the night sky may both be looking at the same collection of stars, but one will see the image of a plough, and the

37

other will make out a dipper. The 'stars' in a literary text are fixed; the lines that join them are variable.   ("Reading Process," 28)

While it is possible to argue over the degree of cultural determination in the reader (obviously an Eskimo would not see a plough), Iser's figure is validated for reapplication to Romantic poetics precisely because it is a model that, whatever its flaws from a purely theoretical standpoint, governs the way in which certain Romantic and Victorian poems are produced.[59] Long poems increase the figurings of the reader by multiplying textual solar systems into galaxies; Robert Browning, in fact, uses exactly the same model in his preface to *Paracelsus* (1835):

> It is certain, however, that a work like mine depends more on the intelligence and sympathy of the reader for its success — indeed, were my scenes stars it must be his co-operating fancy which, supplying all chasms, shall connect the scattered lights into one constellation — a Lyre or a Crown.
>
> (*CW*, 1, p. 65)

"Supplying all chasms," as a metaphor, is I think a more logical term than "bridging" or "filling" gaps. But the figures are for all purposes the same. Browning and others who follow this aesthetic must have faced a number of questions: what kinds of literary works will bring out the intelligence and sympathy of the reader? What genres and styles will ask him to provision himself the most thoroughly for his journey through the text? What is the tradition behind this poetic? Many of the answers, I believe, can be found in the text of *Sordello*.

In an essay on Browning's "Childe Roland to the Dark Tower Came," Harold Bloom notes that for "a Post-Enlightenment poem to begin, it must know and demonstrate that nothing is in its right place."[60] Strangely enough, Bloom's generalization, broad as it is, might be expanded: for works aspiring to an aesthetic of difficulty, "nothing" itself (the "gap") is in the wrong place. Browning's close friend Domett wrote the poet after reading *Sordello*, and suggested that he was "difficult on system" — which Browning denied, suggesting that in living by himself he imaged another portion of his self as audience, and thus neglected the "Stokes and Nokes" of the theatre pit (*RB & AD*, pp. 28-29). The aim of writing for a fit audience, though, includes systematic, tactical difficulty, and in a letter to his publisher when he contemplated a new and more friendly edition of *Sordello*, Browning says, "I shall make it as easy as its nature admits, I believe — changing nothing and simply *writing in* the unwritten *every-other-line* which I stupidly left as an amusement for the reader to do — who, after all, is no writer, nor needs be."[61] What Browning, referring to *Sordello*, calls "the unwritten every-other-line," goes beyond what modern reader-response theory dubs "blanks" or "gaps." Iser describes the communicative asymmetries between text and reader, noting that "the blank is not a given, ontological fact, but is formed and modified by the imbalance ... between text and reader. Balance can only be attained if the gaps are filled, and so the constitutive blank is continually bombarded with projections" (*Act of Reading*, p. 167). As we read and reread *Sordello*, however, we find that the onslaught of readerly projectiles, while filling up one blank, rends the fabric of narration in another spot. Thus Browning's poem veers towards the status of a *text*, in Barthes' sense of a subversive force opposed to generic taxonomies (the *work*). *Sordello* defeats any feeling on the reader's part of harmonious completion, not so much by maintaining an asymmetry between text and reader, as by continually, consciously reminding the reader that such fissures inevitably exist.

The reader is, indeed, the "great idea" which motivates the production of post-heroic poems like *Sordello* in the early-nineteenth century. In the next chapter I hope to examine Browning's original and determined effort to come to terms with Romantic notions of the fit audience and creative reading through an examination of the multiple audiences within *Sordello*.

CHAPTER TWO

Audiences In and
Audiences Out of *Sordello*

I

Lionel Stevenson once titled an essay simply "The Key Poem of the Victorian Age," in order to surprise his reader mid-way with the revelation that the poem to which he referred was Browning's *Sordello*. I would like to argue that the audience of *Sordello*, or rather the audience manqué, might be considered the key audience of the age as well. The decade of the 1830s was full of speculation about the nature of poetic language, and it is worth asking how in this context Browning's poem could so famously fail. Where were the reviewers, who throughout the decade called for greater rigor in poetry, when Browning needed them? In his review of *Philip van Artevelde* in 1836, William Henry Smith calls for "poetry in which the meaning is conveyed at a flash, by bold types and fragmentary efforts of the imagination, bearing somewhat the same analogy to the ordinary language of thought, as symbolic writing to the alphabetic character."[1] A man of this opinion one would think would champion Browning's poem against the reviewers who found it full of "unintelligible oozings" and suggested it be subtitled "'exercises for the asthmatics,' from the wheezy, spasmodic, sobbing nature of the verse."[2] But one of the mysteries of the age is that *Sordello* had no public advocates.

It has usually been thought that Browning brought most of this abuse and neglect on his own head by writing a poem that was simply too difficult for a popular audience to read. But Browning, as the evidence clearly shows, wrote for a "fit audience, though few" of what we might now term the avant-garde. And he wrote first, I believe, for friends such as Amedée de Ripert-Monclar, William Johnson Fox, and Thomas Carlyle. His attitude is explained in a letter to Monclar shortly before the publication of *Paracelsus*:

— Tis an affair of some 4000 lines, done in 3 or 4 months, novel, as I think, in conception & execution at once, &, from its nature, not likely to secure an overwhelming auditory — *you* will make it out easily enough.

(Correspondence, 3, p. 125)

Browning's expectations for his friendly readers were high, and Monclar's lengthy commentary on this poem dedicated to him shows that Browning wasn't disappointed (see *Correspondence*, 3, pp. 416-24). But Browning also writes, I think, for critics such as William Smith and J. A. Heraud who were speaking clearly in favor of the difficulties of Wordsworth, Coleridge, and Shelley and against the easier modes of Byron, Campbell, and Scott. These men prided themselves, like the editor of *Sartor*, on their "tough faculty of reading" (*Works*, 1, p. 221), and would not have balked at a little readerly toil; nor would they have objected in principle to being offended by what they read. We should remember that in Carlyle's final paragraph to *Sartor Resartus* he weaves "a kind farewell" to his "irritated readers" (1, p. 238). In this view, a text should be an irritation like the grain of sand inside the oyster shell, from which some readerly pearl might grow. So why was *Sordello* mocked, abused, and forgotten? — and not forgotten by the general readers, the devotees of L.E.L. and Bulwer's plays, but by the very audience to whom it was addressed with such care? Shortly after publication Browning proclaims in a letter to his friend Macready that the poem was "praised by the units, cursed by the tens, and unmeddled with by the hundreds" (*New Letters*, p. 23). The pattern by which such a work would spread its influence is, as we have demonstrated elsewhere, a commonplace for Browning's generation: the units would spread the word, and eventually the thought would reach the "people." In the words of one advocate of this view, "the book is thus secretly perpetuated, and lives, merely because it *will* be heard."[3]

Browning's tactics in *Sordello* extend this credo: who will may hear the story, although volition becomes not a quality of the text, but an asset in the reader. Browning clearly feels that his poem responds to certain demands of his age; despite its difficulty, *Sordello* is patently a public, not a private, poem. Hans Robert Jauss, in an essay of 1970, makes a clear case for the importance of the audience as a creative participant in the work:

it is only through the process of its mediation that the work enters into the changing horizon-of-experience of a continuity in which the perpetual

41

inversion occurs from simple reception to critical understanding, from passive to active reception, from recognized aesthetic norms to a new production that surpasses them.[4]

Under this view the historicity of literature inevitably entails the form of dialogue; Browning's poetry seeks this form too, as several recent critics have pointed out in work on both *Sordello* and on the monologues.[5] Browning makes the relation to the audience (including the continuing audience of past poetry) central to his aesthetics. Lee Erickson has observed correctly that *Sordello* must be read "as a modernist poem," but is quite wrong when he adds that "without fully realizing what he was doing, he wrote an avant-garde poem."[6] In talking of a writer's aesthetic theories one must assume in the case of self-conscious poets that they are aware of what they are about; Browning's early work is, I believe, a conscious and highly individual effort to direct the reader into a mediative process; it finds its place in a discourse about poetry that is neither typically Romantic nor Victorian, and attempts to make out of the rewards and difficulties of reading an aesthetic that will shape the poetry of the new age.

Sordello is designed to be a first step towards the development of a poetic language that will presumably be a new boon for all mankind (though Browning uses irony to undercut this ultra-Romanticism and thus makes sure we take all such aspirations with a grain of salt). It reflects in a contorted narrative form the competing ideologies of the 1830s, whether in art or politics, and aims not for popular acclaim but for the unexpected "popularity" of Carlyle's *Sartor*. We are still left wondering, however, how a poem that seems to know its audience so well should fail to find even these receptive readers. While it is wrong to think that a triumph among the public was expected, or even desired, it is clear that Browning was disappointed in the reaction of the small group for whom the poem was written. Twenty-three years after the fact, he writes in his re-dedication of the poem to his friend Milsand that "I wrote it . . . for only a few, counting even in these on somewhat more care about its subject than they really had" (*CW* 2, p. 123). To understand why Browning's work proved so unacceptable to contemporary readers, however, it is necessary to look briefly at the question of genre and reader expectations.

Part of the answer to the conundrum of the reception of *Sordello* may be in the choice of a narrative rather than a dramatic mode. In his survey of Romantic narrative, Karl Kroeber notes: "A narrative in which we had to deduce the action, that is the story, plainly would be a contradiction in terms." Kroeber finds that "the Romantics were pleased by the definiteness, the palpability of actions represented through narrative."[7] These statements, which are best applied to writers of popular tales, more directly describe public expectations for any new narrative poem. Mill's comment on Shelley in 1833 reveals a common presupposition about narrative verse: "He had scarcely yet acquired the consecutiveness of thought necessary for a long poem; his ambitious compositions too often resemble the scattered fragments of a mirror; colours brilliant as life, single images without end, but no picture."[8] But Browning contradicts the terms of the narrative by asking us, more or less, to deduce the action, and this cuts against the reader's generic expectations, rubbing preconceived attitudes the wrong way. Applying Mill's mirror image to *Sordello*, the "scattered fragments" of mimesis are there (for those who will) to reconstruct into a picture, which the reader will then suspect is mostly a portrait of himself. It seems, then, that Browning's attempt to have the reader participate in drafting of the constellation of meaning may have been at its most unpalatable for the reader of 1840 when cast in narrative couplets.

The collapse of the market for poetry — which had boomed in the age of Byron — also affects Browning's choices. Numerous attempts to capture Byron's market by dozens of imitative poets had all failed to varying degrees, and Browning develops quite early an unusually strong belief in the necessity of poetic originality. Another option — for those who closed their Byron after 1833 — might be termed the Faustian; Goethe's play was frequently translated and discussed in the 1830s, and Carlyle especially held Goethe the man up for admiration as the very type of genius in the Nineteenth Century.[9] Browning comes close to this mode in *Paracelsus*, which achieved much success at least in terms of critical estimation. But Browning's letter to Sarah Flower Adams when he was hunting for a publisher for *Paracelsus* shows some of the difficulties which awaited the young poet:

on saturday I waited on Murray, or rather Murray's son, & on presenting the kind puff of Mr. S. I learnt, as I had anticipated, that "King Pandion he is dead: & all his Peers wrapped up in lead." i.e. Lord Byron is "no mo" & Poetry "no go." Mr. Fox said much, last sunday, of a Printing-press at work just now in the S. Sea isles... do you think Kokey-Pokey-Whankey-Firm would offer terms? (*Correspondence*, 3, p. 133; 8 April 1835)

Browning didn't have to seek a publisher in the South Seas, but he certainly felt that the crisis in the poetry market was all the more reason to experiment with the forms of poetry; what was there to lose? Tennyson had been hailed as the author of unpopular (hence good) poetry; *Paracelsus* was praised in the same terms; and the success — limited but true — of Carlyle in convincing the public to purchase difficult and stylistically individual works in prose may have provided the model for audience acquisition that Browning needed.

Browning seems to have aimed his poem towards the idea of reader-participation from the beginning, certainly from 1835, when he interrupted his work on *Paracelsus* and penned the introductory statement about the reader's "co-operating fancy" that "shall connect the scattered lights into one constellation — a Lyre or a Crown" (*CW*, 1, p. 65). This quotation is rapidly becoming one of the favorites of Browning scholars for its insight into his rhetoric, but Browning's "constellation" is itself significant: the lyre or crown denotes the choice between song or power that is the informing gesture of Sordello's story. We may also see here the split between harmonious singing between reader and text, and the principle of mastery (either by reader or writer) that we discussed in connection with De Quincey in the previous chapter.

II

The poet-audience relationship functions on three levels throughout the poem, and these may be imagined as broadening out, like concentric circles. In the innermost one we find Sordello coming to grips with the problem of being a troubadour poet and finding a median between the "people" and the privileged audience of noble princes whom the troubadour serves; this may be said to constitute the plot of Browning's narrative. In the next circle we encounter the narrator telling the poem to his conjured audience of ghosts (fellow poets). Very closely aligned with this frame is the outer circle, the historical Robert Browning and his Victorian readers, including personal friends such as Euphasia (Fanny) Haworth who are inscribed into the poem. This last audience, ironically, brought the poet-audience interchange to a level Browning could not have foreseen: rather than filling in the gaps in the text, they created a counter-text, the cycle of *Sordello* legends which usurped the poem's place in the age's estimation.

In order to explore fully his hypothesis about the poet-audience relationship, Browning needed the extra distancing available by having three poet/speakers at work: Sordello, the narrator, and himself. One of the problems of the poem, however, arises from this structure: the narrator and the author are not, as in the contemporary fictional edition *Sartor Resartus*, clearly separated.[10] It is thus assumed by some that the voice speaking the poem is personal and even "confessional." A recent biography of Browning sums up *Sordello*, Browning's "last long adventure on the sofa of self-analysis, carrying therapeutic examination to its logical extreme of privacy and complication."[11] But Browning signals his distance from the narrator in the first paragraph of the poem, through an allusion in which the speaker compares himself with Don Quixote standing on a hill, imaginatively transforming the dust kicked up by two flocks of sheep into armies. The clear indication (the headline printed in 1863 is "A Quixotic attempt") is that the author is thus analogous to Cervantes — and clearly aware of the follies of the Quixotic narrator who will attempt to resurrect Sordello from history's murk.[12] It is the narrator's attitude towards his audience that I will examine first.

We are aware from the beginning that the narrator speaks with diminished authority, especially when compared with the tradition of the epic poem into which Browning's poem overtly moves itself. He is talkative and questioning of his audience — which at this point we assume is confined to readers — and warns us of the role that we must expect to play:

> Only believe me. Ye believe?
>   Appears
> Verona... Never, I should warn you first,
> Of my own choice had this, if not the worst
> Yet not the best expedient, served to tell
> A story I could body forth so well
> By making speak, myself kept out of view,
> The very man as he was wont to do,
> And leaving you to say the rest for him.   (I, 10-17)

The narrator would delight in being both poet and audience — though not in Mill's sense of the poet singing to himself. His position is more analogous to that of the editor of *Sartor Resartus*. Confronted with the disorganized scraps of Teufelsdröckh's history, the editor declares: "Biography or Autobiography of Teufelsdröckh there is, clearly enough, none to be gleaned here: At most some sketchy, shadowy fugitive likeness of him may, by unheard-of efforts, partly of intellect, partly of imagination, on the side of Editor and of Reader, rise up between them"

45

(*Works*, 1, p. 62). The narrator's task of disentwining Sordello from the chronicles and the shadow of Dante is a kind of paperbag task, and he expresses a wish to sit with his readers and watch Sordello "rise up between them" — he being "not a whit / More in the secret than yourselves" (I, 23-24). But the speaker, for a number of reasons, cannot do this; he must wield a "pointing pole" (I, 30) for an audience faced with "unexampled themes" (I, 26). Who is the speaker imagining himself to be here? The action of chalking "broadly on each vesture's hem / The wearer's quality" (I, 28-29) makes the reference to a tailor likely — albeit of a metaphysical kind that links the narrator to the clothes philosophy of Teufelsdröckh: "What too are all Poets and moral Teachers, but a species of Metaphysical Tailors?" (*Works*, 1, p. 231).[13] As a poet, Sordello indulges in tailoring of this kind, as the narrator mocks him in Book V over his fantasy of Rome: "those you'd feast there want the knack / Of keeping fresh-chalked gowns from speck and brack" (63-64). The tailor's chalk-marks, though, are guides to be used in refitting the clothes, and I think that these must be read by the reader, who must then complete the garment from the pattern of the text.

The writer's task, then, is to reclothe the past — but I will look more closely at the relationship to Romantic historicism in the next chapter. For now, I will focus on the notion of the reader's "co-operating fancy," which is demonstrated in part by using an inscribed audience as a pointing pole for the real audience of readers. Modern narrative theory can here be useful.

Part of the novelty of *Sordello* is Browning's idiosyncratic use of the device of the inscribed audience, or the "narratee." Not all narratives are equipped with overtly discriminated built-in audiences (though all can be said to characterize, in some fashion, their readers).[14] Peter Rabinowitz has redefined the idea of the narratee in a recent essay, and he notes that the narratee is "someone perceived by the readers as 'out there,' a separate person who often serves as a mediator between the narrator and the reader."[15] This mediation is often, especially in eighteenth-century fiction, an example of how-not-to-read; it is this traditional use of the device which Browning expands. A precedent may be found in Carlyle's use of the "Editor" in *Sartor*, which doubles the mediative process, and allows for exemplary corrections, since the editor-as-misreader can realize his deficiencies and then teach the narratee:

Or, cries the courteous reader, has your Teufelsdröckh forgotten what he said lately about 'Aboriginal Savages'.... No wise courteous Reader! The Professor knows full well what he is saying; and both thou and we, in our haste, do him wrong. (*Works*, 1, pp. 46-47)

Another of Browning's friends of the 1830s provides an example; in *Captain Sword and Captain Pen* (1835) Leigh Hunt inserts these lines in brackets after a graphic and gory description: "[Oh! shrink not thou, reader! Thy part's in it too; / Has not thy praise made the thing they go through / Shocking to read of, but noble to do?]"[16] Browning's use of multiple discriminated narratees, however, raises the ante of complexity; the "courteous reader" is no longer merely an image of conventionality from whom the (ideal) reader will learn, by negative example, how to respond. Gerald Prince distinguishes some features of texts which pay attention to the narratee through what he terms "overjustifications":

Narratives in which explanations and motivations abound...are very different from those in which explanations and motivations play a limited role.... The former are often by narrators who find the dimension of discourse (*discours*) more important than that of narrative (*récit*) or who are acutely aware of the gratuitousness — and even falseness — of a certain type of narrative and consequently try to exorcise it.[17]

Browning's narrator, from the opening allusion to Cervantes, wants us to be aware of his discourse before we are cognizant of the story (*récit*) he will attempt to tell us. While the action of Sordello's story begins, as an epic should, *in media res*, the more important action of the making of the poem is foregrounded first, and should also be seen, perhaps, as a middle point in the narrator's discourse about his own project.

The narrator's raising of an audience of ghosts who are fellow poets is thus an important action, perhaps the key strategy in his struggle to begin. He defines them early in Book I:

> My audience: and they sit, each ghostly man
> Striving to look as living as he can,
> Brother by breathing brother; thou art set,
> Clear-witted critic, by... but I'll not fret
> A wondrous soul of them, nor move Death's spleen
> Who loves not to unlock them. Friends! I mean
> The living in good earnest — ye elect
> Chiefly for love — suppose not I reject

Judicious praise, who contrary shall peep
Some fit occasion forth, for fear ye sleep,
To glean your bland approvals.   (I, 49-59)

Like much of *Sordello*, this passage is structured to defeat underreading
(sleeping) and to compel rereading. Many listener/narratees in Romantic verse seem to be on the verge of sleep — Byron's "Mazeppa," Moore's
Lalla Rookh, and the first version of Tennyson's "Morte D'Arthur"
provide a few examples — but Browning's audience is an active one of
poets (excluding Shelley, whose "pure face" the narrator banishes in
lines 60-64), and these are by definition men awake to the world. The
presence of the brother-poets may be glossed by a sentence from
Shelley's *Defence*: "the jury which sits in judgement upon a poet,
belonging as he does to all time, must be composed of his peers: it must
be impanneled by Time from the selectest wise of many generations."[18]
Browning however leaves the judicial notion latent at this time, though
as we shall see he has spelled it out in *Paracelsus* and will recur to it in
Sordello. Calling these poets "brothers" adumbrates the notion of fraternal speech which is an important part of Sordello's program in Book V
(see lines 635-37), and the fear that his friends will fall asleep is justified
in Book VI, when the speaker interjects: "but, friends, / Wake up" (VI,
873-74). Finally, in this list of the things one could not see in the lines
above upon a first reading, the fit occasion for peeping forth occurs in the
last half of Book III, when the speaker (at this point conflated with
Browning through a series of personal references) pauses to muse about
his poem-in-process.

   Browning's audience, however, is not often collectively addressed; the
"you" seems not plural, but singular, though not always properly
named. For instance, when the narrator takes a dramatic tour of Goito
castle, the "you" seems to point to a combination of a previous epic hero
and his creator:

                    Why strange
        Such a recess should lurk behind a range
        Of banquet-rooms? Your finger — thus — you push
        A spring, and the wall opens, would you rush
        Upon the banqueters, select your prey,
        Waiting, the slaughter-weapons in the way
        Strewing this very bench, with sharpened ear
        A preconcerted signal to appear;

> Or if you simply crouch with beating heart
> Bearing in some voluptuous pageant part
> To startle them.   (I, 317-27)

Odysseus and the suitors are alluded to here, and the alternative to slaughter — to crouch, observe, and create a pageant — may be the task of Homer. (Though poetry-as-pageant also denotes the aesthetics of ease.) Once again the theme of a choice between song or deeds, lyre or crown, is placed before the reader, who also must invent a connection between the ancestor-poet, the epic situation, and the current poem-in-progress. This readerly work-order destabilizes almost all usage of the second person pronoun in the poem.

Elsewhere in Book I, the speaker instructs the narratee(s) to construct his (or her or their) own descriptions:

> Yourselves shall trace
> (The delicate nostril swerving wide and fine,
> A sharp and restless lip, so well combine
> With that calm brow) a soul fit to receive
> Delight at every sense; you can believe
> Sordello foremost in the regal class   (I, 462-67)

The implication is that the audience believes what they have themselves traced, and the parenthesis, as so often, may imply ambiguity of voice: we may be hearing the narratees' tracing of Sordello's appearance, not the speaker's self-interruption.

It is in Book III, however, that the narrator's interaction with his audience comes to the fore, and Sordello's story is completely halted. This digression is the crux of the poem's relation to its audience on all levels, and it has drawn a greater degree of attention from critics than other portions of the poem.[19] The distance between speaker and "Browning" has narrowed since the poem's dramatic beginning; in Book II after the speaker describes Sordello's rival he states: "So much for Eglamor. My own month came; / 'Twas a sunrise of blossoming and May" (II, 296-97), and it is no secret that Browning was born in May. So when in Book III they encounter the line, "I sung this on an empty palace-step / At Venice" (III, 676-77), commentators are quick to remind us of Browning's trip to Italy in 1838 to visit the locale of his poem — though Browning himself states in a letter that he "did not write six lines while absent."[20] Browning's headnotes added in 1863 help to depersonalize the speaker at this point, but in 1840 Browning clearly means the distance to collapse, much as Byron means to disintegrate the

49

figure of Childe Harold in the last two cantos of that poem. In *Sordello*, this metatext spawns not only commentary on the poem, but also parallel narratives, allusive parables, and deictic references that realistically site a place of narration for the first time (the opening address takes place in a no-place and no-time). Despite these precise details, reminiscent of the innovations of Romantic conversation poetry, the digression progresses through the use of "tactical" difficulty, in which, in Steiner's terms, the "underlying manoeuvre is one of *rallentando*.... There is a dialectical strangeness in the will of the poet to be understood only step by step and up to a point."[21] Browning rounds off the poem, but the sphere must be completed by the reader; it is important then, at this circle-completing juncture, to investigate what has happened to the gathered audience.

Some of them, at least, seem to be already asleep, if we can find a reference to them in a line which also refers to Sordello and Palma: "They sleep, and I awake / O'er the lagune" (III, 614-15).[22] The speaker then ponders the possibility of rededicating his poem to an attractive Paduan waif he spies under an arch, dangling her feet in a canal. She is rejected in the flesh and re-presented as a "sad disheveled ghost" (III, 696), a personification of suffering humanity, to whom he then addresses a highly metaphorical harangue; the poet-ghosts of the past have been replaced, for the moment, by a personification of the anonymous many. The situation is explained later in Book III, in the lines to "Eyebright." The speaker says, "the sad / Disheveled form wherein I put mankind / To come at times and keep my pact in mind" renews him (III, 968-71). This rejuvenation takes the form of a rededication of the poem to attend to common humanity, as represented by the girl, now sleeping (we assume metaphorically) upon the poet's shoulder. But this rededication is ironically undercut by what comes next, a long discussion of poetics, with exemplum given of various genres of poems. If the audience for this bewildering and complex section is still the Italian waif, it is amusing (and deconstructive of the speaker's discourse) to think of her napping through such a formidable lecture in a foreign tongue. More importantly, as Browning's narrator turns "clear witted critic" of his own endeavor, it may be an ironic example of the attention usually given (and perhaps deservedly so) to analytic criticism. Clyde de L. Ryals' understanding of the poem's ironic mode is most helpful when tackling this digression; he notes that *Sordello* "becomes more penetrable ... when one recognizes it as one of the supreme examples of ironic art. For the poem has as its chief subject the impossibility of writing the kind of poem its author would like to write and yet is, at the same time, a brilliant example of the type of art to which it aspires."[23] Browning's revealment of the poet's dense articulation of poetics to the "proper you" (suffering humanity) who can never understand anchors this irony at the midpoint of the poem.

Browning makes a last shift in Book III when the speaker turns to soothe a portion of his original audience: the living in good earnest. He does this, characteristically, through the associative power of a parable, one that plays on the guest/parasite/host tension in the relation between writer and audience. Browning has just directly challenged the auditors: "Have ye times, places, actors of your own? / Try them upon Sordello once full-grown" (III, 937-38) — and his allusion to an exploit of Hercules comes next:

> If Hercules first parched
> His foot in Egypt only to be marched
> A sacrifice for Jove with pomp to suit,
> What chance have I? The demigod was mute
> Till at the altar, where time out of mind
> Such guests became oblations, chaplets twined
> His forehead long enough, and he began
> Slaying the slayers, nor escaped a man —   (III, 939-46)

The writer is imaged as the foreigner who, according to the story out of Herodotus, must be sacrificed in order to end a famine in the land; the heroic writer (like Ulysses and the suitors, alluded to in Book I) is able to reverse the situation, overcome his muteness, and slaughter the slayers. There is a neat reversal of a customary figure here; poets are usually imaged as biblical prophets (rather than muscular heroes) who are outcast or ignored and forced to endure contumely in their native land. Sterling pictures Carlyle in this role in 1839 using terms that also reverberate throughout *Sordello*:

Amid the clamorous snarl and gossip of literature, and the dead formulas of superficial science, here sounds a true prophetic voice, which the best of the dead might throb to hear. Nor will it be without fit audience among us, who, for want of living prophets to slay, have only tried to abolish the memory of the old ones, save as pageant figures for adorning shrines which they would have called down lightning to devour.[24]

The fit audience here seems to be an ironic play on the usual fate of prophets — a fate that abetted the ancient development of dark tropes and hidden allegory. Browning's story of Hercules carries the idea a step

51

farther, imagining the revenge by the hero-as-prophet on the audience. But if even the "fit audience" is dead, the writer's deed loses its validity; the traditional struggles (and the metaphors that illuminate it) have no winners here. Clearly the readers must award their chaplets to the writer without the intent to then sacrifice him to their customs, and the writer in turn must not lead the reader to some linguistic slaughter. Metaphor and allusion have predictably derailed communication, and the speaker must now interrupt to prevent misinterpretation of the tale: "Take not affront, my gentle audience! whom / No Hercules shall make his hecatomb / Believe, nor from his brows your chaplet rend —" (III, 947-49).

The provisional nature of the work has been indicated throughout by continued exhortations to "believe." The audience, which has been sleepily with him from the beginning (when they were "fresh-chapleted to listen" — I, 25), is now addressed by the speaker in an attempt to convince them of the need for *Sordello*. Two living friends in particular, W. S. Landor and Fanny Haworth, are singled out, for different reasons. Landor represents for Browning the exceptional recognition of his work by a member of the band of Romantic poets, one whose first poems were published in the 1790s, and whose friends or acquaintances numbered almost all of the major Romantics. Browning says to Landor (alluding to the story of Polycrates in Herodotus), that he would fling the prized jewel into the sea, "content / Wearing your verse in place, an amulet / Sovereign against low-thoughtedness and fret!" (III, 964-66). Landor's own verse, it might be added, wilfully ignores publishing concerns; much of it was privately printed, and a good bit was composed in Latin. This address to Landor raises a thematic concern too, one that is inevitably ambiguous, given Sordello's opportunity to become Salinguerra's warrior-heir at the end of the poem. In the first Book Shelley is banished, at least in part because of the incompatibility of his "pure face" with poets who were also men of action: Aeschylus (Browning alludes to his participation in the battle of Marathon), and the soldier Sir Philip Sidney. Landor is yoked into the fold as a poet of this group, "Whose great verse blares unintermittent on / Like any trumpeter at Marathon" (III, 951-52) — and a meeting with Landor under the eye of Sicily's Mount Aetna is recalled, when towards the volcano "tilting cloudlets prest / Like Persian ships for Salimis" (III, 958-59). Landor himself had enlisted with the Spanish against Napoleon, and found ways to serve both the cause of poetry and liberty. At this juncture Browning may be weighing his own options: given not only the Italian waif but the "Condition of England" (Carlyle's "Chartism" appears in 1840) what might be the point of finishing the poem? Landor's encouragement of Browning to find his place in the poetic Valhalla helps propel him to the end.

With Fanny Haworth, Browning acknowledges the importance of the personal friend as audience instead of the public recognition of the precursor. Miss Haworth had made an imaginative response to *Paracelsus*: five pen and ink sketches (reproduced in *Correspondence*, 3, p. 250). More importantly, the two sonnets in the *New Monthly Magazine* addressed "To the Author of 'Paracelsus'" by Haworth marked a high point for Browning. At the moment of poetic questioning in Book III, with the audience nodding and suffering humanity unserved, we may sense in the background of the invocation to "Eyebright" her estimation of Browning's assurance and her faith in his future achievements:

> He hath the quiet and calm look of one,
>   Who is assured in genius too intense
>   For doubt of its own power, — yet with the sense
>   Of youth, not weakness, — like green fruits in Spring
>   Telling rich Autumn's promise: — tempering
> All thoughts of pride, he knows what he hath done,
>   Compared with the dim thrill of what shall be
>   When glorious visions find reality,
> Is like an echo gone before, — a tone
>   When instruments would prove their harmony
> Before the strain begins, — a rain-drop lone
>   From the storm-laden cloud. Unconsciously,
>   Perchance, his musing spirit is the guest
> Of future ages, who shall prize him best.[25]

Haworth's poem praises potential more than achievement, and the potential of an unfinished poem haunts Book III; earlier Browning has turned to a "you" and sympathized with the reader's plight: "Alas / For you! who sigh, when shall it come to pass / We read that story, when will he compress / The future years, his whole life's business, into another lay" (III, 643-47). Browning in following the raindrop of *Paracelsus* with (he hopes) the storm burst of *Sordello* uses this sonnet in a talismanic way in *Sordello* III. Haworth's receptivity for Browning's work was clearly predicated on her personal fondness for the author, and she thus stands in for all lovers — friends and family — members who support the poet. Many of these readers responded directly to Browning's work with works of their own — Monclar's commentary on *Paracelsus*, for example, or the extensive marginalia with which Domett filled his copies of

Browning's works.[26] Christine Froula reads the addresses in Book III as "a most ambiguous homage to Landor's *Idyllia Heroica*," and says that Browning impolitely challenges Haworth's notions of poetry with a "gibing address."[27] But I think that Browning's nod of thanks to Landor is quite sincere, and it is surely a severe misreading of both the poem and the evidence of Browning's near love affair with Fanny Haworth to imagine that the tone is anything other than friendly recognition, or perhaps playful teasing.

To this special (loving and creative) audience, the narrator (now, at least to these friends as they recognize themselves, Browning *in propria persona*) explains how poetic visions are inadequate: "Each a God's germ, but doomed remain a germ / In unexpanded infancy, assure / Yourself, nor misconceive my portraiture" (III, 982-84). To illustrate the perils of misprision, or rather the readerly inactivity that will keep the poem in prolonged infancy, we are given what the 1863 headnote will call "a story to the point." The fable, about John of Patmos, illustrates the line "What seems a fiend perchance may prove a saint" (III, 989). Browning here warns the audience against easy interpretation; as Herbert Tucker notes of this tale: " 'The point' is Browning's rigorous demand for a patient reading of his poem."[28] It is a warning that is repeated in the lines about a snuffing civet at the end of the poem. This recognition of inevitable misinterpretation is balanced by a confidence in the "fit audience though few" such as Landor and Miss Haworth, who "elect for love" even if they do not at first comprehend. We should keep in mind, however, that Browning is not annoyed by opposition, but by easy admiration; in a letter to Elizabeth Barrett, Browning alludes to *Sordello* when he explains that "what I laughed at in my 'gentle audience' is a sad trick the real admirers have of admiring at the wrong place — enough to make an apostle swear" (*Letters of RB and EBB*, 1, p. 19; see also *Sordello*, II, 621-24). But the point may be that the poet must be willing both to be called a fiend in order to be named, at a later reckoning, a new kind of saint, and gratefully acknowledge admiration for the wrong reasons.

Sordello can be divided neatly in half, and this tale of John of Patmos gives the speaker the impetus to enter the second half of the poem. The human feeling called into play by the Paduan waif, coupled with the reminder that the true poet needs only a few readers (a doctrine repeated, ironically, by even the most unabashedly popular poets of the 1830s) restores a unity of thought and feeling, and makes possible the graphic realism of Book IV. The transition is made through a more confident and emphatic version of the opening line of the poem: "The puckered brows unfold — / And you shall hear Sordello's story told" (III, 1021-22). The remainder of the poem shows a more confident speaker, and one who makes fewer and less nervous comments to the inscribed audience.

The narrator's confidence, however, evaporates by the end of the poem as the poem itself circles back to its beginning, and the audience once more snoozes. It is at this moment that the poem's final anecdote — the revelation of the boy of Asolo presenting a snatch of Sordello's first song for the delectation of Nature herself — ironically heralds an all-powerful singer, Pippa, who makes an effect without an awareness of an audience at all. The speaker, though, his words now terminating in sleeping ears, must question the efficacy of verse. He awakens the audience in order to signal that the poem is over; he is uncertain in his own mind as to its worth: "but, friends, / Wake up; the ghost's gone, and the story ends / I'd fain hope, sweetly" (VI, 873-75). Confirmation that this is but a hope comes in the final lines; the question is put to the audience: did *Sordello* leave them with the smell of a perfume or a stink? And the answer is ambiguous: "friends be frank: ye snuff / Civet, I warrant: really? Like enough — " (VI, 879-80). Civet, however, is both a foul musk *and* an ingredient of perfume. A passage from *King Lear* perhaps gives us the true meaning; Lear is raving to Gloucester about the dual nature of womankind:

> But to the girdle do the gods inherit, beneath is all the fiends'. There's hell, there's darkness, there's the sulphurous pit; burning, scalding, stench, consumption. Fie, fie, fie! pah, pah! Give me an ounce of civet, good apothecary, to sweeten my imagination. (IV, vi)

What seems a fiend may prove perchance both fiend and saint, or merely human. Browning's audience may feel as mad as Lear by the end of this strangely aromatic poem, or at least disposed to descry the "sulphurous pit" of difficult incomprehensibility in Browning's verse. The reference to "civet," then, should help readers realize that *Sordello* is a strong snuff designed to sweeten the imagination and instigate an "after-gust" of action. But this can be assured only by a willingness to participate: "Who would has heard Sordello's story told" (VI, 886). Finis.

III

Within the poem's frame, then, the speaker and his audience have not fared well in their relations; they enact a play-within-a-play that may symbolize the loss of the popular audience for the long poem in the early-nineteenth century. But the speaker's creation, the poet Sordello, fares even worse, as he never quite grasps that the question of the poet's "Proper you" which he attempts to resolve is in fact not answerable. His progress as a poet is in four stages, with each one marking a different approach to the problem of the audience.

From the moment his consciousness awakens, Sordello is engrossed in life and joyful. His is the boyhood of "genius," and part of Browning's purpose is to deflate the cult of genius prevalent in the late-Romantic era, when the bard is exalted as "representative of Genius — Imagination — Fancy! Human creator! partaker with Deity of his most incommunicable attribute!"[29] The description of the boy Sordello in his idyllic setting might easily fit into Isaac D'Israeli's "Youth of Genius" chapter in *The Literary Character*.[30] Worshippers of genius are also satirized in the person of Naddo, who is introduced during a moment in which reality intrudes upon paradise; the speaker then remarks, "Not a circumstance / That makes for you, friend Naddo! Eat fern-seed / And peer beside us and report indeed / If (your word) Genius dawned with throes and stings" (I, 692-95). It should be noted that the narrator's request to Naddo to "peer beside us" places him in the conjured audience rather than in the poem itself — or, it makes his type simultaneously present. Naddo can certainly be read as a figure of the 1830s (John Forster some say); as we find out in a humorous revision of 1863, "only Naddo's never gone!" (V, 1012 — in 1840, the line ends "Naddo's gone!"). But while the "fern-seed" never-never-land of the cult of genius is one of Browning's primary concerns, he is more deeply interested in the relation of the poet/genius with the total audience. This issue is incorporated into the poem both on the personal level of the interplay of self and other, and on the social and political level through an analysis of the interaction of leader and crowd.

The time thus comes early for Sordello when he must consider other people, and the potential audience: "what informed the boy / Others desired a portion in his joy?" (I, 685-86). Sordello's first "crowd" is the entirely imagined one of subjective fantasy: "Amid his wild-wood sights he lived alone: / As if the poppy felt with him!" (I, 704-05). In this he fits the pattern of the poetic boyhood which Byron puts into the voice of Tasso:

> It is no marvel — from my very birth
> My soul was drunk with Love, — which did pervade
> And mingle with whate'er I saw on earth:
> Of objects all inanimate I made
> Idols, and out of wild and lonely flowers,
> And rocks, whereby they grew, a Paradise,
> Where I did lay me down within the shade
> Of waving trees, and dreamed uncounted hours.[31]

Beginning with the edition of 1822, this passage is quoted by D'Israeli in his "Youth of Genius" chapter, and Browning, in his review of Wilde's book on Tasso (the "Essay on Chatterton") calls for greater research into "the wondrous youth of Tasso" (*CW*, 3, p. 163). Sordello assumes this prototypical development (one that Browning clearly associates with his own boyhood in Camberwell), and then progresses from communion with the fauna around Goito to an imagined mimetic world of "Lord, Liegeman, Valvassor and Suzerain" (I, 768).

This crowd is a figment of Sordello's creativity, and for a time he rules this world like a god; as Aprile in *Paracelsus* sees, "God is the PERFECT POET, / Who in his person acts his own creations" (II, 648-49). Sordello acts his creations, which he terms "puppets" (I, 800), but the more he specifies this crowd in his mind, the more they tend to assume autonomous existence. This unreal audience is constructed by Sordello through a series of questions. The first is, "Whence contrive / A crowd, now?" (I, 747-48), and in the lines that follow the unindividualized multitude is given form, through study and language. Sordello begins with "the entire out-world" (I, 757), which comes into focus as "A stream of life-like figures through his brain" (I, 767). The next question, which is sprung on the reader abruptly, is, "But as for gazing, what shall fix that gaze?" (I, 771). The harder one gazes, seemingly, the more the object seems to break away; the crowd now begins to assume its own life, the individual members "stand each alone" (I, 776). Sordello describes this phenomenon with a metaphor of counterfeiting, of letting "foreign recognition stamp / The current value" (I, 787-88). Here the rate of exchange (in poetry, the terms of critical reception) determines the worth of the text, but what is received in gold is transmuted into paper, stamped or signed by the audience, and consequently (if not absolutely counterfeited), devalued or deflated.

Sordello's fantasies are now shaped and driven into works of language: "so must speech expand the dumb / Part sigh, part smile" (I, 796-97), and Sordello:

> Betakes himself to study hungrily
> Just what the puppets his crude fantasy
> Supposes notablest, popes, kings, priests, knights (I, 799-801).

These puppets are a "marshalled flock / Of authorised enjoyments" (I, 806-07), and they are the first fruits of Sordello-as-author (I think the pun is Browning's). But the more deeply he studies men, projecting himself into the place of crusading knights and the like, the more he is drawn to realistic assessment. At this point though he is satisfied to rehearse improbable futures, and returns (the speaker's mockery creeping in), "as to the moon / From earth" (I, 826-27).

Sordello's dream creations, albeit moony, represent an ideal of unity in which poet, poem and audience are one. The narrator ironically dubs this desire "Apollo."[32] Sordello's first acquaintance with poets now begins, not from books, but from wandering troubadours and trouveres, singers with the useful function (exploited, we find out later, by Salinguerra) of news-bearers and propagandists for the Ghibelline cause. This phase culminates in his love for Palma, which effectively reduces the "gaze" to one focal point, and he now decides to engage in "the veritable business of mankind" (I, 1000).

The poetic condition of the age — the factor of the horizon of expectations — affects the modes in which the young Sordello must create. Sordello's first "performance" comes in a *tenson* with the troubadour Eglamor, and results in his being named Palma's minstrel. According to Simonde de Sismondi, "the *tensons*, or *jeux partis*, were songs, in dialogue, between two speakers, in which each interlocutor recited successively a stanza with the same rhymes," and the example he quotes is a *tenson* between Sordello and Bertrand d'Alamanon.[33] Browning thus introduces his poet in the act of practicing the most interactive of genres, one in which the listener (reader) must create a poem or risk some personal loss. This risk-taking genre, defunct in the nineteenth century, may be another example for the inscribed audience, who are struggling or sleeping with Browning's poem. The two poets squared off for combat are also, of course, types for Browning's own day.

In the competition with Eglamor, Sordello is faced with a poet who "lived Sordello's opposite" (II, 195) — a poet who is in love with the perfection of his art rather than his ability to change the perceiver of his art. Sordello's first song, however, because it is the response in the *tenson* to Eglamor's initiating verses, begins his career within the idea of poetry represented by his "opposite." Herbert F. Tucker states that "Eglamor is naively devoted to a poetics of complete correspondence between fixed form and fixed meaning."[34] For Eglamor, the common notion of Naddo is correct, "And Verse a temple-worship vague and vast" (II, 197). It is a notion which in the 1830s, under the guise of exalting the artist, actually contributes to placing him in a subsidiary sphere, far from the operations of power. Sordello himself wastes time attempting to be perfect, like Apollo; in his speeches, the narrator's sarcastic interjections, such as calling him "Dear monarch" (II, 415), are timed to break in whenever Sordello's discourse heads towards Naddo's notion. The post-Romantic interest in a sort of up-dated religious sublime exalts the figure of the artist, who must work perfection within the area of art, segregated from that of action. (In speech-act theory, these poets would strive towards pure "constative" rather than "performative" utterance.) Besides the reigning Byronisms, a "vague and vast" school of poetry develops in Browning's day with the astonishing popularity of Pollok's *Course of Time* (1828), and the pictorial grandiosity of Martin's biblical paintings as canvas equivalent. (It is later termed the "Spasmodic School," and gets a sendoff to match its own hyperbole.) Worshippers credit the poet with performative powers that are beyond belief, and the net result is the easy acceptance of poetry that leaves the audience unaffected, unmoved, and (finally) uninterested. Naddo, who sums up all nonsensical poetics (and thus "Only Naddo's never gone!"), makes just this point:

> as well you hid
> That sense of power you have! True bards believe
> Us able to achieve what they achieve —
> That is, just nothing — in one point abide
> Profounder simpletons than all beside:
> Oh ay! The knowledge that you are a bard
> Must constitute your prime, nay sole, reward!   (II, 814-20)

Browning's distaste for the concept of the bardic is centered in fact on the nothingness of achievement, on the powerlessness of the bardic cloak and utterance; the periodic prattle of the 1830s is full, though, of hyperbolic claims for the "power" of just such poetry, and the actual effect of such verse is patently zero. Browning wants instead to test language that through its difficulty will actually be performative; a kind of test is represented in Book II, when Sordello debates poetic issues, and visualizes a poet who will "vex / With no strange forms created to perplex" (II, 435-36) his audience. After this speech, the narrator sums up impatiently: "Song, not Deeds, / (For we get tired) was chosen" (II, 440-41).

Sordello's *volte-face* from the position of song as inaction comes, significantly, when he returns to Mantua and faces an adoring crowd:

> Then he found
> (Casting about to satisfy the crowd)
> That happy vehicle, so late allowed,
> A sore annoyance; 'twas the song's effect
> He cared for, scarce the song itself: reflect! (II, 482-85)

While he is swayed by homage, it is praise for the wrong reasons; Sordello sees the nullity of this type of song, and retreats to reform his vehicle, or language itself. Once committed to this course of audience orientation, he paradoxically loses his audience. When he returns, Sordello exclaims, "Accomplished! Listen Mantuans! Fond essay!" (II, 587), but they listen, like the audience in an initial reading of *Sordello*, with great difficulty: "Lacks / The crowd perceptions? painfully it tacks / Together thoughts" (II, 595-97). A great deal of weight lies here on "perceptions." While the tacking of thought to thought is the normal process by which literature is reconstituted in the reader, defined, in Iser's terms, as "synthetizing an assembly of constantly shifting view-points" (*Act of Reading*, p. 97), Sordello wants "perception," an ability to compass thought, not string it together. Romantic poetics insist on the extra-linguistic, suprasensible nature of poetry, and thus privilege poetry as a category of sensible language that exceeds its limits. Browning makes a real innovation here with the Sordello story; making poetry in the vernacular is one task, and making a vernacular which is a vehicle for a new kind of consciousness is quite another.

Browning thus pushes the Sordello story, as presented to him in the chronicles, into the context of his own day and a program for the development of poetry. In this stage of Sordello's relationship to his audience, the story is most closely aligned with his role as a forerunner for Dante, whose name is associated in English minds with the powerful trope of language-forger; Dante was re-introduced to the English public in Giuseppe Baretti's essay of 1755, in which he speaks of Dante as the poet "Among the Italians called 'il padre della lingua e poesia tuscana,' 'the father of Tuscan language and poetry.'"[35] By Browning's time this view had become almost a cliché. As Macaulay writes in 1824:

> Dante adventured first. He detected rich treasures of thought and diction which still lay latent in their ore. He refined them into purity. He burnished them into splendor. He fitted them for every purpose of use and magnificence. And he has thus acquired the glory, not only of producing the finest narrative poem of modern times, but also of creating a language.[36]

The metaphor of language-forging, like most striking things in Macaulay's prose, is hardly original. In *Sordello*, Browning takes this familiar imagery of language-smelting and wrings it through every change to show — not the victory — but the victory-inducing failure of the poet who comes before. The narrator, who is self-confessedly involved in a similar project, is perhaps most deferential to Sordello while describing how he "slow re-wrought / That language, welding words into the crude / Mass from the new speech round him" (II, 574-76). The failure of this project with the Mantuans is, in a way, a rehearsal of the potential for failure of the narrator's own *Sordello*, and it may have been meant to defuse the reaction to Browning's own reformation of the vehicle of English verse.

This version of the poet's attempt to change his audience at a very basic level, the vehicle of thought itself, speaks to the high Romantic ambitions of silent, gradual, but total change at some fundamental core, as well as a more pragmatic approach to poetry which calls for greater compression in order to distinguish more sharply by style the matter and import of a long poem from the narrative of prose fiction. Sordello's next approach to his audience involves something quite different, the attempt by the poet directly to influence the power struggles of his time by using his persuasive power upon an era's "chiefs." Browning examines here a key component of Carlyle's thought in the 1830s.

Browning before 1840 came under Carlyle's tutelage to an extent that has never been adequately measured. Carlyle certainly has a more direct impact on *Sordello* than does Shelley, and it is worthwhile to examine briefly the quality of this relationship. Carlyle and Browning began moving in the same circles around 1835, when both were acquainted with William Macready, Leigh Hunt, and others. It was at Hunt's in April of 1836 that the two first met; Browning's green riding coat gave Carlyle the impression that he was (in Browning's words) "a poor scribbling-man with proclivities for the turf and scamphood" (*New Letters*, p. 263).[37] Both Browning and Carlyle were recipients of copies of Marianne Hunt's bust of Shelley (though with different levels of enthusiasm), and both were welcomed into Covent Garden under Macready's management.[38] The friendship was certainly strong by 1841, when we have Carlyle's first surviving letter to the poet. Like many young men of the time, Browning regards Carlyle as a mentor, and the key years for this relationship are just at the moment of wrapping up *Sordello* and sending it off to the press. The friendship, in fact, was probably more extensive than the surviving records show. Many references by Browning in later years indicate the depth of his gratitude to Carlyle for his guidance in the period from 1838 to 1845. In a letter to Elizabeth Barrett, Browning writes that "I know Carlyle and love him — know him so well, that I would have told you he had shaken that grand head of his at 'singing,' so thoroughly does he love and live by it" (*Letters of RB and EBB*, 1, p. 26). Three letters of Browning to Carlyle from widely separated years all make the same case: "We [Browning and Elizabeth] determined that whenever I wrote to you ... it would be wiser to leave unsaid, unattempted to be said, my feelings of love and gratitude for the intercourse you permitted since a good many years now" (1847; *Letters*, p. 16); "Shall I really hear from you, a sincere word such as you helped me with fifteen years ago and more?" (1856; *Letters*, p. 44); "You knew him [Pen Browning] when a child and were kind as he even yet well remembers: he is now some years older than was his father when you were more than kind to / Your grateful and affectionate / ROBERT BROWNING" (1878; *Letters*, p. 183). Browning may have been shy in specifying his debt, but the debt was real and the tone of these comments is unique in the Browning correspondence. In our consideration of *Sordello*, the existence of this personal relationship makes it all the more important to examine Browning's grappling with Carlyle's ideas, especially since he turns them about within the context of the poet's role, and tests them in numerous ways. The most important of Carlyle's notions that Browning injects into *Sordello* is the debate over the role of the individual "hero" in history. Browning attended Carlyle's heroism lectures in 1841, and the ideas he heard were already well known to Carlyle's readers; Carlyle, in a review of Lockhart's *Life of Scott* (1838), succinctly states the heroism doctrine:

> And yet, at bottom, it is not merely our gregarious sheep-like quality, but something better, and indeed best: what has been called "the perpetual fact of hero-worship"; our inborn sincere love of great men! ... Understand it well, this "hero-worship" was the primary creed, and has intrinsically been the secondary and the ternary, and will be the ultimate and final creed of mankind. (*Works*, 29, pp. 23-24.)

Browning places this doctrine in question by opposing the workings of the leader or chief to the mass movements of the crowd. The opening allusion to *Don Quixote*, in fact, neatly asks if we can "believe" in any "hero" singled out from a common herd of sheep. Like Carlyle's discussions, Browning's analysis is based on the revolutionary events of the 1830s, an era of powerful "people's" movements and weak ministers, when even the great hero Wellington proved ineffectual against the wave of sentiment for Reform. Lawrence Poston notes that "while Browning appears to have agreed with Carlyle that revolutions were sometimes necessary, his poetry shows something of Carlyle's belief that such upheavals seldom bring out the best in those who enact them."[39] Much of Browning's early work is comprehensible only if we detect the undercurrents of metaphor and analysis that shift the foci from the romance of the past, to the act of making poetry in the present, to the politics of that act within a revolutionary era.

It is within this context that we should read Sordello's third attempt at reaching an audience, which involves a role as privy counselor to Salinguerra, a powerful "chief." By approaching this single ear, the poet's song may succeed in effecting change where it could not when addressed to the "crowd." But all of Sordello's encounters with Taurello are loaded with irony, from his first failure to appear to sing at a fete for the leader at the end of Book II. After the retreat to Goito caused by this nonappearance, Sordello is brought out of retirement by Palma, whose manipulations after the death of Adelaide show her to be a true daughter and behind-the-scenes craftsman. At Ferrara, Sordello makes one last dream vision, a fantasy of a perfect Rome, but he is propelled by the gruesome realities of the siege to give up this Romantic fantasy (discussed in greater detail in the next chapter) in order to focus on an act of persuasion.

Sordello's dream-poem in Book IV comes crashing down because of the nature of his audience: "Ferrara's squalid sons" are brutalized by war, and the speaker must ask Sordello at the beginning of Book V, "Are this and this and this the shining ones / Meet for the Shining City?" (9-11). It is one of the significant intersections with Dante's text, because it is after Virgil's recognition of Sordello as a fellow Mantuan that Dante begins his digressive polemic against the constant warfare of Italy's city states:

63

But those who are alive within you now can't live without their warring —
even those whom one same wall and one same moat enclose gnaw at each
other. Squalid Italy, search round your shores and then look inland — see if
any part of you delight in peace.[40]

Dante and Browning associate Sordello with Italy's warfare, and the
hard fact of this warfare in Sordello provokes an overnight dream of
"Rome," similar, as we will explore in the next chapter, to Dante's
hopes for Italian unification.

The major portion of Book V, however, deals with the ramifications of
Sordello's public banishment of his idealisms and dream-performances,
and his finally discovering an audience. First, however, he must be
himself the audience for the message of a "low voice," a kind of delphic
inner oracle:

> Thou archetype,
> Last of my dreams and loveliest, depart!
> And then a low voice wound into his heart:
> Sordello (lower than a Pythoness
> Conceding to a Lydian King's distress
> The cause of his long error — one mistake
> Of her past oracle) Sordello, wake!
> Where is the vanity? Why count you, one
> The first step with the last step? What is gone
> Except that aëry magnificence —
> That last step you took first? an evidence
> You were... no matter. Let those glances fall!
> This basis, this beginning step of all,
> Which proves you one of us, is this gone too?
> Pity to disconcert one versed as you
> In fate's ill-nature, but its full extent
> Eludes Sordello, even: the veil's rent,
> Read the black writing — that collective man
> Outstrips the individual!   (V, 78-104)

This extraordinary passage is one of the key places in the poem, though
it has received little comment, perhaps because Browning's later extensive revisions overdetermine its meaning.[41] An archetypal vision attempts to situate the poet's vision beyond the temporal and the fragmentary; it is countered, then, by the message of the low voice, though its
dangerous, oracular quality is underlined by the allusion to the "Pythoness,"
whose advice (notoriously) is studied in its ambiguity. (The admission of
oracular error, though, may refer to the dubious attempt to be Apollo of

Sordello's youth; as a part of the process of entering the world after the Apollohood of Goito, "by degrees / The Pythons perished off; his votaries / Sunk to respectful distance" — I, 927-29.) The voice links Sordello finally and irrevocably with the people; it serves as a speaker for some collective unconscious realization of the intersubjective nature of human endeavor. The "black writing" — both dark and emphatic and unwelcome to the poet-as-god — is that the totality of human culture outweighs any single contribution; the low voice's exemplum of the motto is a description of poetry in which one bard follows another, all building up, brick by brick, the poetic tradition. The rending of the veil that marks the final transcendence here renders that ascent a descent into the collectivity. It does not follow, of course, that any given brick is inconsequential and nugatory. Some must be cornerstones, the timing and placement of which make the edifice possible.

Browning's own position as a writer in the 1830s can be reconsidered here; in an era in which poetry seems to be a dying art, in which publishers discourage young poets or ask them to foot the bill for their books, the paradigm for the poet seems most often to be that of a creator-god. At the same time, the explosion of literacy and publications designed to exploit relatively uneducated readers meant that, for the first time, writers had a chance to reach the masses directly. Browning had already met a young man his age whose *Pickwick Papers* and *Oliver Twist* seemed to be universally popular. If the "black writing" must be read, then, it must also paint a new picture of an audience for the poet. Through Sordello, Browning renounces the grandiose poet-god and the easy verse of narrative (novelistic) tales as well, and embraces the difficult, epical poem that follows the paradigmatic "fit audience though few" road to the people. Sordello's descendental crash in Book V leaves the poet with few, but realistic options. But first, at the conclusion of the speech of the "low voice," the Pythoness (merging now into the ironic tone of the speaker) directs Sordello to persuade Salinguerra of the justness of the Guelph cause:

> Since talking is your trade,
> There's Salinguerra left you to persuade,
> And then —
> No — no — which latest chance secure!
> Leapt up and cried Sordello: this made sure,
> The Past is yet redeemable whose work
> Was — help the Guelfs, and I, howe'er it irk,
> Thus help! (V, 301-07)

Sordello jumps again to the end, to the ultimate redemption of the Past which no one action can redeem; his canceling of the low voice's "And then" with his own resolution to convert Salinguerra to the Guelf party is a more practical step than dreaming of Rome reborn, but the "voice" has more to say, and its wisdom is lost.

Sordello's first speech to Salinguerra, who ironically hails him as "Elcorte's happy sprout" (V, 311), is completely fruitless:

> The contrivances to bind
> Taurello body with the Cause and mind
> — Was the consummate rhetoric just that?
> Yet most Sordello's argument dropped flat
> Through his accustomed fault of breaking yoke,
> Disjoining him who felt from him who spoke: (V, 329-34)

Sordello, as in the break-up after his experiment with language fails, experiences a disassociation of sensibility, and with this flat, rhetorical pleading he has no chance to influence Salinguerra, who merely wonders that the youthful poet is prematurely aged. Sordello continues, while Salinguerra contemplates, ironically, turning Guelf as a ploy to trap his enemies. He then bursts Sordello's bubble by reminding him of the time when Sordello refused to sing for his entertainment: "Not that I see where couplet-making jars / With common sense: at Mantua we had borne / This chanted, easier than their most forlorn / Of bull-fights, that's indisputable!" (V, 410-13). This scorn prompts Sordello's second speech, a visionary poetic one which is the opposite of his consummate rhetoric. Sordello here seems finally to have found the "will" as well as the "vehicle" and the proper "you." He is, in short, on the verge of being a Carlylean Hero, such as Joan of Arc, as Carlyle describes her in his early *Life of Schiller* (1825): "she goes forth on her mission; all bends to the fiery vehemence of her will; she is inspired because she thinks herself so" (*Works*, 25, p. 157 — but in *Sordello*, Thinking doesn't necessarily make it so). Isobel Armstrong has found that in *Sordello* "'Will' is Browning's word for the imagination."[42] This is certainly true, in that only those with imagination "may hear Sordello's story told," but the term implies more than the customary meanings of the imagination, even in its exalted Romantic usage. It conveys, I think, a sense of mind reacting, empowering, moving in the world: as Hazlitt put it, "Thought depends on the habitual exercise of the speculative faculties; action on the determination of the will."[43] At this point in the poem, poetry truly merges into action, and the imagination becomes one with the will.

66

Sordello's speech is itself his greatest poem, but its effect on the audience is unpredictable, and it is now that the narrator puts himself back in the foreground, cutting against the divine afflatus of Sordello by asking what will be the effect if a troubadour goes

> So far as to conceit his knack or gift
> Or whatsoe'er it be of verse might lift
> The globe, a lever like that hand and head
> Of—Men of Action, as the Jongleurs said,
> —The Great Men, in the people's dialect?   (V, 423-27)

The reference to the "Great Men" here seems to bring the thought close to Carlyle again, though the speaker's ironic implication is that a "knack or gift" will not be able to lever in a new age. Yet the "dialect" is the right one in which to speak, and Sordello has a genuine opportunity, at a moment in which the people seem to be striving for a voice, to make a difference. This conjunction of the liberal cause of the people's inalienable rights with the elitist necessities of the poet's craft is, I think, close to Browning's heart, and underlies much of his poetry in the first half of his career. It is connected to the poetic that theorizes a perfect poem only in non-linguistic apprehension. Sordello's conception broods "unexpressed and whole" (V, 436) in an ur-state in which the poem is perfect and omniscient; the moment after, words come forth, and the product is inevitably deformed by expression in language. But the processional and fragmentary nature of verse is balanced against its degree of novelty, the degree to which the novel utterance has reacted upon the lever of the future: Sordello does manage, after all to make "for that age, a novel thing" (V, 455). The problem is to find the style that will be able to express the new without being totally incomprehensible. In the Chatterton essay Browning defines how Genius first attempts to "compete with, or prove superior to, the world's already recognized idols, at their own performances and by their own methods" (*CW*, 3, p. 165). Confidence thus gained results in the end of imitation and the beginning of creation. The poet/genius thus outstrips his race, and must be tracked by others:

And surely, when such an Adventurer so perishes in the Desert, we do not limit his discoveries to the last authenticated spot of ground he pitched tent upon . . . but rather give him the benefit of the very last heap of ashes we can trace him to have kindled.   (*CW*, 3, p. 179)

Browning here makes less idiosyncratic the metaphor from *Sordello*, Book III, in which the poet is the engineer of an elaborate and experimental machine, one which is perennially being constructed just out of reach of the imitators; the speaker here tells another poet:

> So long: and while thou turnst upon thy heel
> Pray that I be not busy slitting steel
> Or shredding brass upon a virgin shore   (III, 857-59)

Sordello's progression then has shown at this moment the utter necessity of originality in art, the poetic brinkmanship that leads to the making of poems just beyond, but in sight of, the grasp of the audience; they are "means to an end / The Many Old producing some One New / A Last unlike the First" (V, 444-46).

The speaker's ironic intervention on the behalf of Sordello, then, places the problem in 1840, when after ten years of mass movement politics the whole question of a people's dialect (or "charter") is charged with ambivalence. Browning's concern, I think, is with the mechanisms by which difficult writers, by their choice of medium excluded from the mass public, might still speak for and to the people and their concerns. In Book II, Sordello has followed Naddo's poetics of give-the-people-what-they-want by imitating Eglamor; in the critic's words, "the Master certes meant to waste / No effort, cautiously had probed the taste / He'd please anon" (II, 495-97). This craven solicitation of the public is rejected for truer service to the people in the shape of poetry that is "for that age, a novel thing." In Book V the final conversion is staged within an interior drama that includes the "low voice" — both conscience and inspiration — and a peculiar kind of audience. For it is at this point that he draws a ghostly audience around Salinguerra, Palma, and himself: "And round those three the People formed a ring" (V, 456). These are brother poets inscribed by the speaker come to judge, as well as Sordello's own personifications of suffering humanity.

The circle of faces gathered here, the result of Sordello's heeding of the "low voice," reverberates throughout Browning's early poetry. It is the audience won through willing the imagination into a contest, a *tenson*, with the famous dead; Browning here is Harold Bloom's precursor. But in *Sordello*, with its insistence on the cause of suffering humanity, this audience also includes "the people." Browning's obsession, though, is with the way the new poet must force his way into the canon, and the other versions of this confrontation — particularly in *Paracelsus*, "Pictor Ignotus," and "Childe Roland to the Dark Tower Came" — may help us grasp the situation here in Book V. Paracelsus, in scene 5, conceives of the confrontation only in terms of fame. The precursors are only enemies, determined to insure that his after-fame is that of a quack:

> What have I done? you dare ask that? or *you*,
> Brave ones? Oh, *you* can chime in boldly, back'd
> By them; and what had *you* to do, wise peers?
> Only observe! why, fiends may learn from them!
> How they talk calmly of my throes — my fierce
> Aspirings, terrible watchings — each one claiming
> Its price in blood and brain; how they dissect
> And sneeringly disparage the few truths
> Got at a life's cost; they too hanging the while
> About my neck, their lies misleading me
> Their dead names browbeating me!   (V, 158-74)

Paracelsus makes an attempt, of course, to expunge the past, to begin again outside tradition. In poetry this would be unthinkable. (Browning's revision of this passage makes clear what is only implied when he adds the lines "Here stand my rivals; Latin, Arab, Jew / Greek join dead hands against me: all I ask / Is, that the world enrol my name with theirs" — V, 161-63). In his delirium, Paracelsus cannot see the natural reason for the dead hands of the past wishing to deny his place on the role of famous scientists and doctors: his own attempted parracide of their fame. The case in "Childe Roland," however, is different. There the band gathered at the end of the quest are peers in a quest in which all fail; presumably the act of failing will inscribe Childe Roland with them on the dubious hillside, ranged round the dark tower awaiting the next candidate for their ranks. It is a negative canon — whether, as Bloom would have it, the Romantic poets or no.[44]

The poem that may shed more light on *Sordello* however is the little regarded "Pictor Ignotis," Browning's first monologue spoken by an artist, which first appeared in *Dramatic Romances and Lyrics* (1845). Here we find a painter who, unlike Sordello (who spawned legends, lives in the *Commedia*, and survives in a scrap of the Goito lay), has completely disappeared into time, become part of collective history only. His is a love/hate relationship with fame, and he ironically asserts his will even to the extent of bidding "die my pictures! surely, gently die!" (*CW* 4, p. 166). The key factor is his reaction to the postulated future reception of his work; He finds the idea of surviving on earth in his paintings "wildly dear! / But a voice changed it"; the voice, as in *Paracelsus* and *Sordello* is followed by a circling of faces:

> This world seemed not the world it was before:
> Mixed with my loving trusted ones, there trooped
> ... Who summoned those cold faces that begun
> To press on me and judge me? Though I stooped
> Shrinking, as from the soldiery a nun,
> They drew me forth, and spite of me ... enough!
> These buy and sell our pictures, take and give,
> Count them for garniture and household-stuff,
> And where they live needs must our pictures live
> And see their faces, listen to their prate.   (45-53)

If Paracelsus feels oppressed by his great precursors, the exact opposite is true here; ambition towards the new is defeated by the imagining of a lowest common denominator audience in the future. What an artist produces is seen only through the eyes of the consumer of products, and an unwillingness to tolerate the "people" leads to a denial of the possibility of art.[45]

When we return to *Sordello* we find a far different state of affairs; Sordello has already passed the stage of the "Pictor Ignotus" in his monologue in Book III (93-221) in which he resolves to "die" because he cannot reconcile himself with the Mantuan consumers of his art. "Convention, hazard, blindness" all contrive to stifle his art (III, 203), says the speaker, but this art is made only for his self. The real audience, though, is suffering humanity, and the faces in *Sordello* are both the representations of the people — as defined by the Venetian waif of Book III and the wretched of Ferrara under siege — and the "great men" or gathered poets who have come to see if Sordello can make use of his splendid opportunity to change history. Sordello parlays with Salinguerra and Palma,

> And round those three the People formed a ring,
> Suspended their own vengeance, chose await
> The issue of this strife to reinstate
> Them in the right of taking it —   (V, 456-65)

Sordello recognizes the proper audience here (in 1863 Browning added six lines to define them as "visionary judges whose award / He recognized in full" — 457-58), and the confidence expressed in the doubling of canonical aspirations with speaking for the people, combined with an inspired loss of self-hood, leads to his most brilliant performance. In truth, Sordello's power has grown, since, however small a step, he has in fact stepped beyond his age; but the people are also there to judge the step Sordello does *not* take. His powerful speech proves him a "hero," and for the people, Sordello "must be proved their lord ere they exact / Amends for that lord's defalcation" (V, 466-67).

Despite Browning's addition in 1863 of the interjection, "Why, he writes Sordello!" (V, 620), which we can read in a number of retrospectively ironic ways, Browning is sincere in his attempt to show how the poet must be responsible in some way for political effects. Sordello says of the poet of the future,

> —but his work is still
> For faces like the faces that select
> A single service I am bound effect,
> Nor murmur, bid me, still as poet, bow
> Taurello to the Guelf cause, disallow
> The Kaiser's coming —   (V, 654-58)

These "faces" urge the poet to work for "humanity" in whatever way is possible, and at this moment (also a moment in the 1830s?) what is possible is persuasive political action. But Sordello's paralysis has meant that his moment is past. Salinguerra, like the narrator's audience, is nodding (V, 559), and when he wakes up at Sordello's peroration, we find that the effect is completely different than the intention; Salinguerra is only flattered to be the recipient of such eloquent energy, and what is worse, he now has new hopes to avoid peace, which has seemed inevitable after Ecelin's withdrawal and the betrothal of Palma to a Guelf. Sordello has proved an "unacknowledged legislator," but from the wrong side of the aisle.

Sordello's conscious desire to do good for mankind, in short, comes up against the hard rock of Salinguerra's will. Carlyle's thoughts on the great man in the "Essay on Scott" again may be of service:

> Far be it from us to say that a great man must needs, with benevolence prepense, become a 'friend of humanity;' nay, that such professional self-conscious friends of humanity are not the fatalest kind of persons to be met with in our day. All greatness is unconscious, or it is little and naught.
>
> (*Works*, 29, pp. 36-37).

Sordello's greatness only occurs with a loss of self-consciousness, when he is able to make his best song and become a "novel thing":

> A reason why the phrases flowed so fast
> Was in his quite forgetting for the time
> Himself in his amazement that his rhyme

> Disguised the royalty so much: he there —
> They full face to him — all yet unaware
> Who was the King and who...   (V, 468-73)

At this moment, at the possession of this idea, he transcends his age. Sordello has been mocked enough by the speaker for his aspirations to Apollohood or Kingliness that at first it is hard to credit the sincerity of these lines, but I think the potential of the evolutionary forerunner is important. In the Scott essay, Carlyle goes on to say that "A great man is ever, as the Transcendentalists speak, possessed with an *idea*" (p. 37). It is ironic, of course, that Sordello's "idea" that makes him a "king" is that great men — especially the traditional practitioners of force — don't count for much against the pressure of the democratic sea. But Carlyle even makes this idea the core of Napoleon's heroism: "Napoleon himself, not the superfinest of great men, and ballasted sufficiently with prudences and egotisms, had nevertheless, as is clear enough, an idea to start with: the idea that Democracy was the Cause of Man, the right and infinite Cause" (p. 37). Sordello's quest for the "proper You," then, has aligned itself with a powerful transhistorical cause that motivates poet and politician alike, sometimes without their conscious awareness. The surfacing of this ostensible end for society (or the people) circles all potential audiences, including the audience of the future, around a moment that is pregnant with possibility.

The final stage of Sordello's career is also the shortest; with the discovery that he is Salinguerra's son, the possibility of direct action opens up for the first time. It is here that rhetoric gets its greatest display, and the poet must become audience to his audience. The objective Salinguerra is a poet too: "He strung the angelot; / Made rhymes thereto" (IV, 612-13), and the speaker has earlier made an interjection to point out he is "A man who shamed Sordello (recognize)" (IV, 593). But he loses his perfections when he begins his own "song" (V, 896) and chants a powerful prophetic litany of all the places they will conquer together. The potential is here for the repetition of the pattern in history — widely noted in Browning's day — defined by the Professor of History at the University of London: "the personal interference of the people, as society is now constituted, almost unavoidably ends in placing a master over their heads; in establishing a despotism."[46] Sordello's moment of destiny has come, and his reaction to Salinguerra's spoken plans will be the key. But while Sordello's speech only moves Taurello to the impulsive action of tossing the Emperor's baldric around Sordello's neck, this speech of Salinguerra's literally kills Sordello:

> And Salinguerra's prophecy at height —
> He voluble with a raised arm and stiff,
> A blaring voice, a blazing eye, as if
> He had our very Italy to keep
> Or cast away, or gather in a heap
> To garrison the better —   (V, 982-87)

Sordello is stupified by this proto-fascist display, and Salinguerra must continue his exuberant *Salinguerriad* to Palma alone. After Sordello's death, the narrator states, "Sordello's inability to bar / Rivals the stage, that evening, mainly brought / About by his strange disbelief that aught / Was to be done" (VI, 756-59) leads directly to the accession to power of the "Grey wizened dwarfish devil Ecelin" (VI, 764). I think that we should understand that Sordello had to act once the baldric was offered to him: Browning condemns Sordello for rejecting the office.

Sordello's failure at this moment may have been, once again, a misreading. He is paralyzed by an inability to see the good of any action, and especially actions whose first steps appear to be evil. And Salinguerra's song is not a rational prediction of the future, but an unintentional parody of Sordello's own overarching dream of Rome, shattered previously by reality. Both Sordello and Salinguerra, in their guises as rhetoricians, might heed this command from Sartor:

> *Do the Duty which lies nearest thee,*" which thou Knowest to be a Duty! Thy second Duty will already have become clearer."   (*Works*, 1, p. 156)

These are words that Salinguerra has lived by but seems to have forgotten. It is after Salinguerra's reply to his "consummate rhetoric" (his first persuasive attempt) that Sordello "knew the truth: / So fantasies shall break and fritter youth / That he has long ago lost earnestness, / Lost will to work, lost power to express / Even the need of working!" (V, 363-67). Salinguerra, though, is seduced by an unexpected destiny, a falsely teleological explanation for his life, and he alters his normal, pragmatic (heroic) procedures. After finding out that Sordello is really his son, he sniffs providence at work: "I tell you towards some such design / Have I worked blindly, yes, and idly, yes, / And for another, yes — but worked no less / With instinct at my heart" (V, 854-57). But it is perhaps important only that he has worked at what he saw as his Duty nearest him, and one of the ironies of the poem is that Salinguerra, who seems so well-qualified to be a leading figure, ends exactly as his son does, subsumed within the orbit of another: "spite of all the schemes / Overt and covert, youth's deeds, age's dreams, / [Salinguerra] Was sucked into Romano" (VI, 671-73). Sordello's greatest poem, then, has as unpredictable an effect as might be imagined. The people's champion is revealed to be the heir to a "chief," or oppressor of the people; Sordello has hitherto idealized poetic explorations into his self-nature, but it is only by becoming un-selfconscious that his nature is completely laid bare. The listener turns poet in his own right, and aspires so mightily that he, like Sordello, becomes incapable of taking any valid short term steps to ward off the ascent of the evil Ecelin. If this is song's intervention in the world, might there be songs that should not be sung?

IV

As a poet, Sordello's need to affect an audience has brought him closer and closer to the sphere of power; caught in the center, he wears the badge of power himself, but dies. (His death, by the way, is not so improbable as it at first might seem, coming as it does after constant traveling and no sleep for three nights.) The narrator suggests that what Sordello has "found" (VI, 603) is the position he rejected when he began his career as a poet: "can his spirit go the mighty round / At length, end where our souls begun?" (VI, 604-05). The return to the point of origin might imply that the answer may be found in the Temple of Art that is Goito and Sordello's boyhood, or, since the line changes in 1863 to "end where poor Eglamor begun?", in the practice of "Sordello's opposite." But the poem does not validate Eglamor's way, only the notion of poetry's importance. For Eglamor, poetry "looped back the lingering veil / Which hid the holy place" (II, 199-200). Although he is the "neediest of his tribe" (II, 223), his gift of verse, in his own estimation, sets him apart, god-like, from other men. In this version, the poet is exempt from the ways of society, unsullied by political machinations, but also insulated from society's power structure and limited to a function that can do nothing more than entertain. This sort of withdrawal, no matter the attendant satisfactions of being followed by a worshipful train of Naddos, goes against the grain of Browning's thought, as does the suggestion, implicit in Sordello's reaction to the baldric, that the poet directly wield power himself. Instead, Browning moves towards a realization that the poet should help to make men into brother poets; he does not say that all men are poets, but that they can and should be.

74

Readers of *Sordello*, with attention and will, are converted into these brother-poets (though Browning, in his explicit statement of this view in a letter of the 1850s, recants it). Herbert Tucker calls this a "wonderfully human hypothesis that all men and women are artists, secondary to what they would ultimately make of themselves and of each other, living and speaking in a region of energetic difference between their reach and their grasp, between desire and articulation."[47] This region where men are continually forging their art marks Browning's most fundamental congruence with Blake, who finds the city of art, as represented by the spiral design on *Jerusalem*, plate 72, "Continually Building, Continually Decaying."[48] The artist who completely masters his art also petrifies it, like Eglamor (or, later, Andrea del Sarto), yet the artist who cannot produce, like Sordello, is no better. The answer to this polarization may be found in the concept of "brothers talk" (V, 625). Wordsworth notes long before *Sordello* is written that "Poets do not write for Poets alone, but for men," and one way of looking at *Sordello* is to see it as the poem Browning writes to tell other poets this truth.[49] There is a reverse truth here too; after *Sordello*, readers are poets (or those who *will* are), so *Sordello* is rightfully written for "Poets alone." In any case, the poet's task is a Wordsworthian communication with other men and women. Lee Erickson's view, that *Sordello* is a story of a poet's rejection of the competing claims of his fellow men, "and so finally turning to his true audience, God," should be rejected.[50] Browning works in the poetic vortexes of the 1830s, in which some commentators ascribe godlike powers to the poet, while others, like the Benthamites, equate poetry to snooker, and he realizes that full communication — and the new acts of reading entailed — must be the human goal of the poet. In order to relate this truth, he gives his hero the pretensions to divinity ascribed to the poet by the Naddos of the 1830s, and then strikes this pose down in an emphatic manner.

In hearing Sordello's story told, we are exposed to a version of the poet's career which continually places his human frailty before us, mocking the power of his verse as well as the power of the Naddos to proclaim "Genius." Placed against this unflattering portrait of the poet is an honest quest to define a new role for the poet and his audience. *Sordello* is thus a series of provisional stances towards the audience: which one will affect them? The sentimental ideal of the perfect lyric as something overheard immediately gives way to a concept of a more dynamic relationship, one of co-operation. Browning could have tried an older approach, and like the allegorist provide for a split in the audience by a separation of the tale, but Browning's relativism provides each man with some portion of the (divine) poem but none the completed form; to solve the dilemmas he has raised he needs a dialogic process — the inter-action of author and reader that he structures into *Sordello*. Immediately after the "Why, he writes *Sordello*" interjection in Sordello's oration to Taurello this process is described in its ideal form:

> Why fancy how I rose,
> Or rather you advanced since evermore
> Yourselves effect what I was fain before
> Effect, what I supplied yourselves suggest,
> What I leave bare yourselves can now invest?
> How we attained to talk as brothers talk,
> In half-words, call things by half-names, no balk
> From discontinuing old aids.   (V, 620-27)

The "leaving bare" for the investment of the reader's imagination is the mechanism which will convert readers into fellow poets.

The audiences within *Sordello* predict its failure with the audiences without; Mantuan-like Londoners preferred Eglamor verse, or the more easily graspable poems of Alfred Tennyson, or even the "vague and vast" *Festus* of Bailey. In a new view of the literary history of the period, we can see how Browning's failure to reach his audience — the "'fit & few' in the intense meaning" that Elizabeth a few years later flatters him with having (*Letters of RB and EBB*, 1, p. 15) — marks a change in what had been a swelling tide of poetry towards more intellectual subjects. At one point in the 1830s it was thought that the way to save poetry was to expand reader-participation by compressing (or perhaps repressing) the syntactical links and narrative sequence. But when presented with Browning's poem, "for its age, a novel thing," the key audience misses the boat; the poem in consequence becomes, for a time, a derelict upon the sea of literature. In terms of the immediate chain of cause and effect in literary history, *Sordello* is the least important poem of the 1840s. But its effects come later, as twentieth-century poets such as Ezra Pound find in Browning's path-not-taken a way to transcend the limitations of late-Victorian verse.

An analysis of audiences within the poem reinforces our understanding of Browning's keen interest in "communication different" (VI, 600) and the obstacles which prevent it. Browning resorts to many tactics to force the reader to cooperate in the making of dialogue, to play, as it were, the puppets alongside the narrator, and, while many of these tactics may be found in other genres and other eras, their incorporation at such length, and with such precision and compression, in *Sordello*, shapes the genre of the long poem towards greater difficulty, towards a level of reader participation that makes under-reading almost impossible. Through the close analysis of several passages in my next two sections, I hope to show some of the tactics by which Browning in his construction of *Sordello* forces the reader to participate.

CHAPTER THREE

The Past Is Hurled In Twain

"Raise, ye bards of other times," continued the great Fingal, "raise high the praise of heroes: that my soul may settle on their fame." The dark winds rustled over the chiefs. A hundred voices at once arose; a hundred harps were strung. They sung of other times; the mighty chiefs of former years.

—MACPHERSON

Lo, the past is hurled
In twain: upthrust, out-staggering on the world.
—SORDELLO

I

The poems of Ossian, despite Browning's boyhood love of them, may seem like a peculiar place to start a discussion of the way Browning calls up the past for his readers in *Sordello*. This particular passage of *Fingal*, however, offers an unusually exact parallel to the opening of *Sordello*.[1] Before Fingal can sing "the mighty chiefs of former years" he must convoke the concatenated voices of "ye bards of other times." This is a suspiciously accurate account of the way oral tradition works, and the writer with the pen is not required to be so formulaic. But in *Sordello* before "appears Verona" the speaker must have his audience of fellow writers:

so for once I face ye, friends,
Summoned together from the world's four ends,
Dropped down from Heaven or cast up from Hell,
To hear the story I propose to tell.   (I, 31-34)

Browning begins his poem, then, with a double invocation. He must call up "Sordello, compassed murkily about / With ravage of six long sad hundred years" (I, 8-9), and he must simultaneously gather an audience, "few living, many dead" and convince them to "believe." These two rather extravagant gestures are often discussed separately, though the poem twines them together: the past cannot appear without an audience,

78

which includes both the living (few though fit, or at least loving) and the dead, represented by the living texts of the past's writings. This is literally true, since without the presence of Dante, the speaker will have no greater orb from which to disentwine Sordello and thus begin his poem.

This trope of Browning's is boldly placed at the opening of the poem; it is more usual to invoke the synchronic presence of the bards at the end of a poem. In "To William Wordsworth" it is after Coleridge's audition of *The Prelude* that he perceives "a linked lay of Truth":

> Ere yet the last strain dying awed the air,
> With stedfast eye I viewed thee in the choir
> Of ever-enduring men. The truly great
> Have all one age, and from one visible space
> Shed influence! They, both in power and act,
> Are permanent, and Time is not with them.[2]

One also thinks of Keats' fine sonnet, "How many bards." While this concept is not unique to the period, it is of unusual importance to Romantic poetry, and the peculiarity of Browning's opening to *Sordello* can only be read against a background that includes a keen consciousness of the hovering presence of the poetic tradition. Blake too calls the poets together, and writes under the aegis of a textual eternity, of a permanence; and like Blake, Browning uses the past as subject for re-enactment. Blake says, in the imperious voice of the *Descriptive Catalog*: "Tell me the Acts, O historian, and leave me to reason upon them as I please; away with your reasoning and your rubbish. All that is not action is not worth reading." The acts of the past are to be found in its texts, the entire structure of the remnants of history; Browning, even more than Blake, because he does not share Blake's absolute belief that the great events of time occur in "a Pulsation of the Artery," recognizes the textuality of the past, and this places his poem firmly in the context of Romantic historicism.[3] Within this tradition, Browning demonstrates the necessity of "reading" the past in the manner of a poet's creative reading of his sources; a reader must participate in all steps of the process.

Browning's choice of the troubadour hero is usually accounted a reflection of the popular interest in the Middle Ages, and in particular the strong appeal of the poetry and times of Dante. The subject itself is such a likely choice that, famously, Margaret Busk published a Walter-Scottish long poem by the same title in 1837. For a popular readership, the past was not a mode of estrangement, and not abysmal; the curtain of the past for most readers was easily lifted: appears Pompeii, says Bulwer, and so it does. (Browning recommended the book to his French friend Monclar — *Correspondence*, 3, p. 126.) The widely read poet Felicia Hemans constantly mined history books (especially Sismondi's) for poetic topics: "Alaric in Italy," "The Troubadour and Richard Coeur de Lion," "The Last Constantine." Many of her subjects would today be described as obscure. It would seem, then, that the formidable amount of scholarly detail in nineteenth-century historical fiction (in both prose and poetry) is structured to make it all that much easier to "believe." Furthermore, the idea of a "window" into the past has important analogues in mainstream genres of painting. History painting obviously opens up the past to view, and during the period in which Browning composed *Sordello*, Turner's popular illustrations in the vignette form to the poems of Scott and Rogers, while landscape-oriented, exploit this motif to illustrate these poets' historical subjects.[4] In literature, a culmination of sorts of the technique of dramatically calling up the past may be found in Carlyle's *Past and Present* (1843). Carlyle tells his reader in this volume what he is doing with the past, and his comments I think shed light on Browning's more oblique method: the historian is an editor, who "out of old books, new Writings, and much meditation not of yesterday . . . will endeavor to select a thing or two; and from the Past, in a circuitous way, illustrate the Present and the Future" (*Works*, 10, p. 38).

Nevertheless, it is often considered part of Browning's failure in *Sordello* that he expects too much from his readers in the way of prior knowledge of an obscure historical background. This is probably not an issue; the difficulty in the poem is not primarily contingent, but tactical (to use George Steiner's classifications). Readers at the time were accustomed to such detail; they had Sordello's era before them in Sismondi and Henry Hallam, as well as Dante (and the detailed notes to editions of the *Commedia*).[5] Many articles on the Italian "revival of letters" appeared in the quarterlies throughout the thirties. This modern rationale for Browning's failure — which Pettigrew defines as "Browning's apparent assumption that his readers would be intimately familiar with the historical background"[6] — is voiced about *Strafford* as well, but Browning is chastized in the *Edinburgh Review* for choosing a hero whom "we all know" *too* well. From the time of Mary Shelley's *Valperga* (1823) to George Eliot's *Romola* (1863), the public is deluged with tales of the Italian medieval and Renaissance periods.[7]

Browning of course *is* very novel in his handling of his subject; his is perhaps the only complete failure (in terms of immediate sales) of this sub-genre during these years, if we define our group as narratives which include a bundle of details about long-gone Italian princes. The secret to this failure (and success) is in the doubleness of the historical mode. Morse Peckham argues that historicism is a mode of estrangement, but that its practitioners were paradoxically immensely popular. (For Peckham, interest in the past is constant, since history's rhetoric at its most basic is a form of gossip.[8]) Browning's text disallows easy reading and the pleasures of gossip, and the reader is forced into a mode of estrangement; *Sordello* cannot be read without viewing the past with a dubious eye as a "hateful surge" (I, 19). Christine Froula contrasts Browning's language with Dante's, and argues that it "diverges from Dante's in the extent to which it makes history, and not a myth of a divine plan, the foundation of poetic and political authority."[9] This is true, but we must not consider Browning's notion of history as determinate, or offering an alternative plan; he is no proto-Marxist. Browning in fact senses (as does Carlyle) some transcendent Truth at work, but cannot find it embodied in clear form. The view of history which I believe underlies Browning's opening has been succinctly defined by Karl Kroeber:

> The main thrust of Romantic historicism is not towards apocalypse nor transcendence but, instead, toward a dialectical engagement with confusingly open-ended experiences, for experience to a Romantic is, by definition, transitional. So the Romantic with an historical subject is in the position of representing what he recognizes cannot be represented. Or, to use a term again becoming popular, he seeks the sublime, which even Schiller . . . identified as incomprehensible to reason and incomprehensible to the senses, and, therefore, specially evocative of imaginative power. The evidence shows romantic historicism to be part of the aesthetics of such sublimity, specifically, the sublimity not of space but of time.[10]

This hermeneutic sublimity, as Thomas Weiskel dubs it, is evoked by the pastness of the past, by the recognition of its "murkiness" and knowledge of its existence only as the interpretation of ruinous fragments and dubious chronicles.[11] The poet's imagination, with the co-operation of the reader, can re-voice these shards and stage the past as a drama, eternally new. It is an endlessness which is unrelated to the sum total of knowledge available.

Romantic history sees the past as infinitely rewritable, *even if* all the data were known. De Quincey explains in his essay, "Greece Under the Romans":

> What then? The facts *so* understood are but the dry bones of the mighty past. And the question arises here also, no less than in that sublimest of prophetic visions, "Can these dry bones live?" Not only can they live, but by an infinite variety of life. The same historic facts, viewed in different lights, or brought into connexion with other facts, according to endless diversities of permutation and combination, furnish grounds for such eternal successions of new speculations as make the facts themselves virtually new, and virtually endless.[12]

This view of the past obviously provides a rationale for creative reading; as Blake put it, the historian must give "the historical fact in its poetical vigour."[13] Each reader may engage in a dialogue with the past, and Browning includes as one of the inscribed readers of *Sordello* a poet, Walter Savage Landor, who makes his name in the 1820s and 30s with just such imaginary conversations. (As all dedicated readers of Landor's "Imaginary Conversations" know, the past is indeed "virtually endless.") *Sordello*'s narrator tells us plainly that we may do as he has done: "(Yourselves may spell it yet in chronicles, / Albeit the worm, our busy brother, drills / His sprawling path through letters anciently / Made fine and large to suit some abbot's eye)" (I, 189-92; see also I, 298-308). Within the wormholes of the record of the past, the poet re-enacts his text, or plays his "puppets" (I, 72); in the interstices of this performance operates the reader's will, which spells out meaning(s). Browning accepts the responsibility of the historian, described in his essay on Chatterton (1842) as "balancing conflicting statements, interpreting doubtful passages, and reconciling discrepant utterances" (*CW*, 3, p. 179). Browning has a fine grasp on the textuality of the past, on its mode of discourse.

Geoffrey Hartman describes historicism as "the staging of history as a drama in which epiphanic raptures are replaced by epistemic ruptures, *coupures* as decisive as Hellene and Hebrew, or Hegel and Marx."[14] Carlyle, though, points out that most of these ruptures remain unstaged because unknown; one of the earliest published manifestoes of English historicism is his essay "On History" in *Fraser's* (1830): "Our clock strikes when there is a change from hour to hour; but no hammer in the Horologe of Time peals through the universe when there is a change from Era to Era." Carlyle tells his readers to "look with reverence into the dark untenanted places of the Past, where, in formless oblivion, our chief benefactors, with all their sedulous endeavours, but not with the fruit of these, lie entombed" (*Works*, 27, pp. 88 & 87). Browning, with Carlyle's essay and, more importantly, the technique of *The French Revolution* paving the way, stages one such rupture with Sordello as its eponymous hero. He peers into the untenanted past and finds an opportunity for Sordello to be a "chief benefactor." But it is an opportunity missed, though Sordello achieves some measure of unearned fame.

In *The French Revolution*, Carlyle aims to make his reader experience events as they develop, and learn to distrust all reports. He weaves these events to make us toil for our own synthesis. Browning goes further; his tale is six-hundred years gone by, and Verona appears reluctantly. Hence the poets must convene to re-collect what will not be interpreted as a decisive coup in the history of poetry, and we must first toil to re-enact not the tale but the telling. Carlyle's dicta in "On History" that "Narrative is *linear*, Action is *solid*" (*Works*, 27, p. 89) may be taken as the motto for the style of both Carlyle's history and Browning's poem. To reweave the solid conflux of three days is the poet's mind-boggling task, one that finds its echoes in the contemporary moment — by a canal in Venice — as well. Lee Baker compares the historical imagination in Browning and Carlyle, and concludes that they differ in that Carlyle is a romantic ironist and Browning "is not . . . for he does not turn this irony against his own adequacy as an artist."[15] This generalization may be true for *The Ring and the Book*, but it is not true of *Sordello*, in which the speaker is frequently shown to be inadequate before the wormholes of the past, and ironically aware of the impossibility of getting a story told without the complicity of the "proper you." The speaker begins, after all, by declaring that he can see Sordello as clearly as Quixote sees Pentapolin, and he then asks the reader — who knows that Quixote is actually viewing a flock of sheep — to "believe" him. What we believe instead is that the past is recreatable in a variety of ways, including a way which transmutes sheep into heroes.

In *Sordello* there is one passage which illustrates the various approaches to the past, from factual to purely poetic — it is in Book II, after Sordello has returned to Mantua to act the part of Troubadour. The speaker pulls back for a moment to his audience, including the historians, to ponder the question of exactly how much we can know about any phenomenon of the past; Sordello has just decided to "go stoutly on" when the break occurs:

> Ay, and goes on yet!
> You pother with your glossaries to get
> A notion of the Troubadour's intent —
> His Rondels, Tenzons, Virlai or Sirvent —
> Much as you study arras how to twirl
> His Angelot, plaything of page and girl,
> Once; but you surely reach, at last, — or, no!
> Never quite reach what struck the people so,
> As from the welter of their time he drew
> Its elements successively to view,
> Followed all actions backward on their course
> And catching up, unmingled at the source,
> Such a Strength, such a Weakness, added then
> A touch or two, and turned them into Men.   (II, 514-26)

The antiquarian studying the texts of the past is humbled before the actual essence of a past experience — in this case the magic of Sordello's impact upon his audience. Historical research is an inevitable falling short. Sordello's own performance, though, is true history in being a fiction; his poem is described as a narrative of actions retraced to their source, but with a touch or two added. This kind of poetry — an "unreal pageantry / Of essences" (II, 564-65) — is history poeticized, made pleasingly linear, but powerless. It is Walter Scott's historical narrative, or poetry-as-recreation.

With time, historical events rise and fall in prominence. Sismondi interestingly notes that "as time has passed away, our imaginations have invested the Troubadour Knight with new glories. No one has experienced this good fortune in an equal degree with Sordello of Mantua."[16] Sordello's story, made into the yarns about the heroic "Prince Visconti" (VI, 823), becomes in Browning's hands a history for poetry in the 1830s. The allotropic mechanism by which the interpretation of the past changes with the fluctuating needs of the present (and future) is explained in Book V in the lines which precede the oft-quoted definition of "brother's speech":

> To-day
> Takes in account the work of Yesterday —
> Has not the world a Past now, its adept
> Consults ere he dispense with or accept
> New aids? a single touch more may enhance,
> A touch less turn to insignificance

> Those structures' symmetry the Past has strewed
> Your world with, once so bare: leave the mere rude
> Explicit details, 'tis but brother's speech
> We need   (V, 627-36)

With this linguistic future before us, then, the convened audience and the readers must delight in collective labor to make "the dim / Abysmal Past divide its hateful surge" (I, 18-19).

Sordello begins with the past imaged as a dark abyss, into which we all must one day slink; but each survival of the past is also a spark which may be rekindled. The revival of embers happens in *Sordello* seemingly of its own accord;

> What hear[t]
> Have I to play my puppets, bear my part
> Before these worthies?
> > Lo, the Past is hurled
> In twain: upthrust, out-staggering on the world,
> Subsiding into shape, a darkness rears
> Its outline, kindles at the core, appears
> Verona.   (I, 71-77)

The past does not respond to the first call, "Appears / Verona" (I, 10-11), but after the narrator defers to, yet marks his difference from, his predecessors, it does stagger out.[17] Browning's innovation is not in the dramatic calling-up of the past, though there is something deeply incantatory about it. Palma describes Adelaide as a witch historian in Book III, "she held me thus — a clutch / To make our spirits as our bodies touch — / And so began flinging the past up" (III, 387-89). Adelaide's revelations to Palma come down to a secret of genealogy, or patrimony — the speaker's calling up of the past, then, may be an analogous attempt to reveal a true poetic genealogy as well, to scan "the selectest of the wise of many generations" to find a man to be heir to. Sordello, in a sense, is son to Salinguerra because Palma wills it so — after Salinguerra selects him with the baldric, but before Palma recounts Adelaide's revelation. The speaker seems to act his own Palma, and selects his own patrimony. The innovation in the calling up of the past, then, is in the presence within the text of the acknowledged ghosts of discourses: "My audience," says the narrator, come "to see how their successors fare" (I, 48-49).

The audience's curiosity about their poetic successors redirects Browning's historical poem towards the future. The reshaping of the past is implicit in all new poems, and the "successors" are not only new poets, but new guises of old bards. No poet stays the same, nor does any poem. Leigh Hunt reports with approval a remark of Keats's in *The Indicator*:

> Talking the other day with a friend about Dante, he [Keats] observed, that whenever so great a poet told us any thing in addition or continuation of an ancient story, he had a right to be regarded as classical authority. For instance, said he, when he tells us of that characteristic death of Ulysses in one of the books of his *Inferno*, we ought to receive the information as authentic, and be glad that we have more news of Ulysses than we looked for."[18]

Browning, too, gives us more news than we looked for, however ironic it is. A poet's aspiration, not achieved in fact, can become an accomplished deed through the afterlife of his fame. In Book I, Sordello in his proto-Apollo phase dreams of being a kind of "renaissance" hero: warrior, poet, lover, statesman. These dreams "rehearse the future" (I, 845). But while the Sordello of Browning's poem does not realize any of these fantasies, he accurately rehearses the future nonetheless, for at the end of the poem Browning reminds us of an alternative series of Sordello-texts, and thereby underscores the act of textual interpretation which has shaped the Sordello-story the reader is being told:

> The Chroniclers of Mantua tired their pen
> Relating how a Prince Visconti saved
> Mantua and elsewhere notably behaved —
> Who thus by fortune's ordering events
> Passed with posterity to all intents
> For just the God he never could become.   (VI, 822-27)

Browning's Sordello, however, is reconstituted not only from documents, but through the gaps in the chronicles imaginatively read. Like all good biographies, his acknowledges its fictional accouterments. The revelation of the fictional Sordello, a Prince of the Visconti family (more famous, actually, in Milan), reminds us at the end of the fictional nature of the history we have at hand. It makes us see the validity of our own step towards seizing the truth of the poem as much as the truth of the incidents of history related by the historian. This view of history is Browning's most important bequeathal to the modernist long poem, and shapes the early *Cantos*, where the Malatesta saga is played out in a drama of documents and the poet's penetrating imagination.[19] In Browning's *Sordello*, resurrection is occasioned by such things as the overheard snatch of the "Elys" song sung by the boy of Asolo at the end of the poem. Dryasdust history has no match for this vision, and consequently the story "will" be heard by an audience with a co-operating fancy. It is within this historicist context that Browning's final act takes shape. The ghosts of the past vanish, and we are told that we must judge them "peri or ghoul" depending upon whether or not they "vanish in a stink / Or in a perfume" (VI, 875-79). To paraphrase Blake, when it comes to the traces of the past, the nose altering alters all. The poem's structure veers, then, and seems at the end to be like a lengthy parable (a lucid one of "A COCK and a BULL" says Yorick, whom one must suspect is among the conjured auditors). Within its compass we may now include the reader's interpretation of the past, incorporating the memory of reading *Sordello*. We are left with a question to answer: *Sordello* may have been pungent enough to ensure the experience of an "after-gust" (VI, 885). But has it? We can be sure only by rereading; Browning suspends and frames an indefinite ending, marking a space for closure that continues indefinitely. Thus when Browning ends the poem by demanding, "friends, / Wake up" (VI, 874-75), the awakening does not signify an end so much as a beginning. The trace of Sordello's song hangs in the air, and the first "after-gust" might logically be thought to be a wide-awake re-perusal of the poem. It is also a closure, if we consider that these friends are composed partly of the poets of the past, in which we are taught how each authentic poem may be sounded anew; every snatch of song that lives unlocks the past, and *Sordello*, read backwards from this overheard piece of the Goito lay, instructs us in how to read both the tradition of the past, and itself.

Browning's opening, we should recall, implicates this sustaining note of closure in many ways other than the famous near repetition of the opening line. The halting recall of the past, and the inclusion (with the exception of "that pure face") of the constituency of poets marks this as an opening of remarkable authority, not least by the way it immediately transfers responsibility to its readers, encoding them into the text. It also enforces a break with what comes before; Browning's narrator reverses his field several times in order to get started; he even picks up the "pedantic *fescue*" discarded by Shandy so that he can point out his "unexampled themes," and limn the discontinuity with whatever precedes the poem's opening. This would include the ending of what-ever lazy, Mrs. Busk-like tale the reader has been skimming before; the rupture is total because Browning demands that we begin with a new kind of reading act, as well as a new tale. This opening authorizes the treatment of history as the endless fabrication of interpretation, the sublime play of text within text, and the palimpsest-like recombinations of text-upon-text. Carlyle's statement is definitive:

> For though the whole meaning [of history] lies far beyond our ken; yet in that complex Manuscript, covered over with formless inextricably-entangled unknown characters, —nay, which is a *Palimpsest*, and had once prophetic writing, still dimly legible there, —and some letters, some words, may be deciphered; and if no complete Philosophy, here and there an intelligible precept, available in practice, be gathered: well understanding, in the mean while, that it is only a little portion we have deciphered; that much still remains to be interpreted; that History is a real Prophetic Manuscript, and can be fully interpreted by no man. ("On History," *Works*, 27, pp. 89-90.)

II

One of the most oblique treatments of history as palimpsest, though, comes in the atemporal song of Rome that Sordello sings in Book IV; this utopian ode seems an attempt to escape from the nightmare of history that is Ferrara under siege. While "Rome" is a theme in Dante, Browning anachronistically invokes the Romantic context of Rome, and Romantic views of Dante, rather than Dante's actual thought. We must assess, I think, the importance of Rome as a contemporary trope for history itself, for all the ways the past persists in the present, as well as the Romantic cultivation of Rome in poem and novel. Rome figures as the "Eternal City," and thus a representation of the atemporal Ideal, and as the ruinous physical reminder of the passage of time in which cityscape blends with nature to make an architectural palimpsest in which each fragment, to borrow a phrase of Wordsworth's, is "a choice trope / In Fortune's rhetoric."[20] By the 1830s Rome had become something of a mania, and every British traveler, it seems, returns with printable reflections. Lord Morpeth's "Scraps of Italy," for instance, begins "O thou eternal Rome! — for to have been / Is still to be — the world's imperial queen," and his reflective position is typical:

> Then he, who dares to tune this feeble lay,
> In mournful homage of thy mightier day;
> Who, wand'ring mid these scatter'd wrecks alone,
> In thy dread destinies forgets his own.[21]

Rome is the perfect text/palimpsest for the view of history we have been discussing, and Rome, too, is the inevitable subject for endless reinterpretation. And, for men like Lord Morpeth, Roman reflections provide an escape from the grimmer realities of their own day.

The handling of the theme of Rome by Romantic writers, as Jerome McGann has observed, is also a test of Romanticism itself,[22] and Sordello's stab at solving political dilemmas through his song of Rome is Browning's implicit critique of a Romanticism, apocalyptic or utopian, that attempts to evaporate history's contingencies. The convoked audience of poets includes many who have made their own songs of Rome. The key texts that bear on Browning's poem are *Childe Harold IV* (with its attendant volumes by Hobhouse); the book behind Byron's poem, Madame de Staël's *Corinne or Italy*; the numerous periodical treatments of the way that Rome figures as an ideal for other Medieval and Renaissance Italian poets, such as Dante, Petrarch, and Tasso; and the popular treatments of the medieval "Romans" in British fiction, which we may call the "Rienzi" motif, after Mary Russell Mitford's popular tragedy (1828) and Bulwer's bestselling novel (1835). At the moment that Sordello picks up the song of Rome we experience a doubling that conjoins Rome's potential as an always renewable past with the historical moment of Sordello's dilemma and the contemporary potential of Italy's (and England's) future.

The topic of Rome is introduced circumstantially; Sordello arrives at the conclusion that Guelf and Ghibelline divide the world and "whoso shall enlist / With either, ranks with man's inveterate foes" (IV, 941-42).[23] Sordello feels though that he has a destiny, and asks what "If a Cause remained, / Intact, distinct from these, and fate ordained, / For all the past, that Cause for me?" (IV, 950-53). The catalyst now appears when a "watcher" — a former monk who has turned soldier in order to keep his wife — asks Sordello for "The tale of the dead worthy, long ago / Consul of Rome [...] Crescentius Nomentanus" (IV, 955-60). Sordello does not know the name, so the man relates how in his monastery this story was used as an example, and he proceeds to tell it to Sordello. Crescentius' tale as redacted by the watcher is one of a man's reach considerably exceeding his grasp: the Consul's robes are given to Crescentius as a jest, but he misreads the situation and through the power of his mind recreates a Republican Rome "kings styled / Themselves the citizens of." This idea is powerful, and "men too catch / The flame, and Rome's accomplished" (IV, 986-90). This "third party" revolt is squashed by Emperor and Pope, and according to the watcher:

They crucified
Their Consul in the Forum and abide
Such slaves at Rome e'er since, that I — (for I
Was once a brown-sleeve brother, merrily
Appointed) — I had option to keep wife
Or keep brown sleeves, and managed in the strife
Lose both. A song of Rome!   (IV, 994-1000)

The tale of Crescentius may be considered here not only as an example of the perils of re-building Rome in a day, but as a substitute for Romantic treatments of the lost liberal causes of the past. Italy for de Staël and other Romantics is a place without a present, and "the Italians are more remarkable for what they have been and might be, than for what they are." In *Corinne*, when the heroine wins Oswald by taking him on a tour of the ruins of Rome, one of the key moments is at the Castle of St. Angelo, a Roman tomb fortified and made into a prison; she tells her lover how "Crescentius, Arnault de Brescia and Nicolas Rienzi, those friends of Roman liberty who so oft mistook her memories for her hopes, long defied their foes from this imperial tomb."[24] The story of Crescentius is found in many sources, from Gibbon to Sismondi to Hobhouse, and had been the subject of a poem by Felicia Hemans as well ("The Widow of Crescentius"). When Sordello begins to dream of a utopian Rome, he has the failure of Crescentius before him, and the reader of *Sordello* must also consider the failure of Rienzi, a strong man who was advised by a later poet, Petrarch. Each case illustrates one of the central tensions of *Sordello*'s political analysis: to what extent must the "people" rely upon individual heroes (or geniuses) to secure their happiness? The implications for the political situation in the 1830s are obvious; Dwight Culler discusses the pervasive Victorian habit of "drawing analogies between their own age and various historical periods in the past and attempting to understand their problems, and their place in history, in terms of these analogies."[25] The crisis of the Reform Bill had produced such a flood of overt historical analogies that Browning (in *Strafford* and *Sordello*) leaves the analogy undrawn as one more constellation of meaning for the reader to discern. At this point in *Sordello*, when the watcher comes forth with the suggestion of the tale of Rome, references to the present are buried, but the present is nevertheless suggested through a network of half-allusions and significant narrative interpolations.

The introduction of the "Roman" consul Crescentius foreshadows the moment when the Baldric is placed around Sordello's neck by

Salinguerra and he must choose whether or not to wield power. Crescentius's failure (according to the watcher) dooms the Roman people to slavery from his day (c. 990) to Sordello's present 1224. In his poem Browning imagines history moving towards crucial moments where paths diverge; it is worthwhile to think of the implied lineage of Crescentius, Sordello/Salinguerra/Palma, Dante/Beatrice, and Petrarch/Rienzi/Laura. The latter group in particular, when one considers the contemporary interest in their stories, has not received the attention it deserves in relation to Browning's poem. The plot of *Sordello*, in fact, makes the troubadour as much Petrarch's forerunner as Dante's, with Salinguerra the potential Rienzi. Browning's copy of Thomas Penrose's *A Sketch of the Lives and Writings of Dante and Petrarch* (1790) is signed and dated 16 November, 1838, and contains Browning's reference in a note in the back to Sordello, so we know that Browning had Petrarch before him as he finished his poem.[26] Walter Savage Landor's recounting of Petrarch's life in 1843 may be used to point out the similarities. Like Browning's Sordello, Petrarch is born on a night of battle, when his father and fellow exile Dante Alighieri join in an attack on Florence. He is raised in a remote and beautiful spot (like Goito — Landor remarks that "the tender heart is often moulded by localities").[27] He wins his laurels at Rome as Sordello at Mantua. The most important analogies occur, though, when Petrarch's politics are brought up. Landor shows Petrarch acknowledging that "Laura was less than Rome" (p. 37), and upon meeting Rienzi, the restorer of Roman freedom, "the love of letters and the spirit of patriotism united them in friendship" (p. 39). Petrarch exhorts Rienzi to pursue the completion of Roman freedom — he is "endowed by nature with manly, frank, and generous sentiments. Meditative but communicative, studious but accessible, he would have followed... the counsels of Petrarca, had they been given him personally" (p. 41). Landor then makes the inevitable comparison with Napoleon, contrasting Rienzi's treatment of Petrarch with the Frenchman's treatment of Madame de Staël. The failure of Rienzi, like that of Crescentius, dooms the human race; Petrarch regrets his fall, and it "is even still to be regretted by his country. It is indeed among the greatest calamities that have befallen the human race, condemned for several more centuries to lie in chains and darkness" (p. 42).

Browning's "Crescentius" foregrounds the issue of political restoration, and the question of the efficacy of the poet's involvement in politics. It also, I believe, echoes the public involvement with the story of Rienzi, which in turn raises the spectre of Napoleonic "heroism." We might ask, then, how the story of Rienzi was interpreted in Browning's day. Bulwer, as might be expected from a vigorous champion of the Reform Bill of 1832, but also a Whig and aristocrat who values traditional institutions, draws a moral from Rienzi's tale that is appropriate for the 1830s as well:

> I have said that the moral of the Tribune's life, and of this fiction, is not the stale and unprofitable moral that warns the ambition of the individual: — More vast, more solemn, and more useful, it addresses itself to nations. If I judge not erringly, it proclaims that, to be great and free, a People must trust not to individuals but themselves — that there is no sudden leap from servitude to liberty — that it is to institutions, not to men, that they must look for reforms that last beyond the hour — [28]

This might also be a moral for Sordello, who, after hearing a very dubious tale of Crescentius's attempt to revive the glory of Rome by force of personality, launches into his own dream-song of Rome restored. It is in this treatment of Rome that Browning turns to *Childe Harold IV* for reference, beginning, I believe, with the stanza on Rienzi that Bulwer uses as the epigraph for his novel:

> Then turn we to her latest Tribune's name,
> From her ten thousand tyrants turn to thee,
> Redeemer of dark centuries of shame —
> The friend of Petrarch — hope of Italy —
> Rienzi! last of Romans! While the tree
> Of Freedom's withered trunk puts forth a leaf,
> Even for thy tomb a garland let it be —
> The Forum's champion, and the people's chief —
> Her new-born Numa thou — with reign, alas! too brief.[29]

Sordello, like Rienzi, is "the projector of a splendid system which was to restore the freedom of Rome and Italy," and as Hobhouse goes on to note, all such projectors in the early nineteenth century bear comparison with Napoleon.[30]

"Rome," like the ideals of the French Revolution, is corrupted time and time again by the impetus for personal dominance; Sordello, on the grotesque battleground of Ferrara, sees "Rome" as a universal ideal aspired to by all:

> And Rome, indeed,
> Robed at Goito in fantastic weed,
> The Mother-City of those Mantuan days,
> Looked an established point of light whence rays

Traversed the world; and all the clustered homes
Beside of men were bent on being Romes
In their degree; the question was how each
Should most resemble Rome, clean out of reach
Herself; nor struggled either principle
To change what it aspired possess — Rome, still
For Friedrich or Honorius.
                              Rome's the Cause!
The Rome of the old Pandects, our new laws —
The Capitol turned Castle Angelo
And structures that inordinately glow
Corrected by the theatre forlorn
As a black mundane shell, its world late born
— Verona, that's beside it. These combined,
We typify the scheme to put mankind
Once more in full possession of their rights
By his sole agency. On me it lights
To build up Rome again — me, first and last:
For such a Future was endured the Past!
And thus in the grey twilight forth he sprung
To give his thought consistency among
The People's self, and let their truth avail
Finish the dream grown from the archer's tale.   (IV, 1001-31)

Sordello has struggled at the beginning of Book IV to establish his identity in Ferrara ("the more he pried / The less became Sordello satisfied / With his own figure at the moment" — IV, 191-93), and this resolution to make Rome his Cause ends the book on a seemingly resolute note. But the passage, which is a blending of Sordello's thought with the speaker's commentary, undercuts the notion that Rome is a legitimate cause for the poet at this juncture. Rome is a principle of dominance, and as such is sought under both Guelf (Honorius) and Ghibelline (Friedrich) principles. The "Capitol turned Castle Angelo" is a bitter irony — either intentional on the speaker's part, or unintentional on Sordello's, because it is at this spot that both a previous attempt to renovate Rome by Crescentius and a later attempt by Rienzi are squashed. The impetus to recreate Rome, though, makes Rome an "archetype" (V, 78) for all attempts by a "sole agency" — whether that of Sordello, Rienzi, or Napoleon — to succor mankind.

It is at this conflux of two eternities, when the poet senses the teleological implications of "For such a Future was endured the Past," that Sordello makes his most egregious (and short-lived) wrong turn.

The final line, "Finish the dream grown from the archer's tale," is also the final irony, as the "watcher" who tells of Crescentius becomes an "archer" — and Sordello, once more watching events and dreaming, resumes his unrealistic task of attempting to become the archer-god Apollo. (Sordello, we might add, is reputed to be the son of an "archer" but is actually the son of Salinguerra.)

The word that matters now, though, is "arch." Book V opens with a swift deflation of the dream of Rome:

> Is it the same Sordello in the dusk
> As at the dawn? merely a perished husk
> Now, that arose a power like to build
> Up Rome again? The proud conception chilled
> So soon? Ay, watch that latest dream of thine
> —A Rome indebted to no Palatine,
> Drop arch by arch, Sordello!   (V, 1-7)

The arches that drop are the architectural ruins of the dream-vision, echoed later in Salinguerra's counter-song of conquest, in which he exults, "On these we pile, as keystone of our arch, / Romagna and Bologna" (V, 866-67). These arches invoke the Rome of *Childe Harold*, especially the famous lines on the Coliseum, beginning "Arches on arches! as it were that Rome, / Collecting the chief trophies of her line, / Would build up all her triumphs in one dome."[31] Arches invoke the coliseum, that visible reminder of Roman pleasure in violence, and Sordello's archetypal dream invokes the failures of previous o'er-arching attempts by individuals to build Rome in a day, as well as Byron's moody visions of gladiators by moonlight. (The word "arch," in fact, is used eight times in *Childe Harold IV*.) Browning follows the collapse of the dream with a lengthy explosion of Sordello's Rome through a description of how a city is actually built, "successively sewer, forum, cirque — / Last age that aqueduct was counted work" (V, 39-40). This lesson parallels others the lesson of Book II, in which Sordello attempts to build a perfect vehicle for his thought; the architectural metaphor applied to language is embodied in a linguistic dream of architecture. Forster's laudatory essay on *Paracelsus* makes the same point about the earlier poem:

> Paracelsus... was no sturdy Destructive, whose mission is accomplished in the mere leveling of his predecessors' edifice. Paracelsus was rather an Augustus, who only pulls down the Rome he finds "all brick," for the purpose of reconstructing it "all marble."

94

Why, then, did he so egregiously fail? We answer at once — *he failed, because, in his case, the pulling down was effected while as yet the marble was unhewn in the quarry, and the bystanders would not wait beyond the upheaving of a block or two!*[32]

Sordello, of course, doesn't get as far as Paracelsus; he has no real impact at all. Forster, in a commentary that says as much about his opinion of the readers for poetry in the 1830s as Browning's poem, lays the blame for failure on the "vulgar, noisy, impatient crowd," and Browning in *Sordello* exemplifies the manifold ways that poetry cannot exist and do work in the world without a fit audience. Rome cannot be (re)built by a single visionary, but only with the co-operation of the many guided towards the steps for which they are ready. In a social and political climate that includes a tension between late-Romantic glorifications of the poet, utilitarian social advancements that find no place for the poetic, and potential upheavals and agitations for "The People's Charter," Browning attempts to wedge an evolutionary creed that, while deflating the vision of the poet as a melancholy demiurge of the Coliseum by moonlight, argues that historical divergences of utmost importance may still be affected by the actions of the poet.

The dream of Rome, then, raises the eternal city as a utopian ideal while at the same time deflating any hope of seeing its realization in more than a fitful step or two; Sordello is left worse off than before. This detour from the main plot of Book IV — the journey with his "out-soul" Palma to influence events on the behalf of the people — emphasizes the temporal nature of history, its slow development, as well as the inability of the historian to see it except through the fragments or ruins of texts. Browning's sources, though, also include Romantic versions of the song of Rome, and he uses these to foreground the notion that there are moments in which liberty (or the fate of the people) hangs in the balance, could we but know when these moments are. The greatest Romantic utopian poem, *Prometheus Unbound*, was written at Rome, according to Shelley's preface, "upon the mountainous ruins of the Baths of Caracalla, among the flowery glades, and thickets of odoriferous blossoming trees, which are extended in ever winding labyrinths upon its immense platforms and dizzy arches suspended in the air."[33] But Shelley recognizes his "beautiful idealisms" will have no immediate effect, and his Romans, like "Ferrara's squalid sons" remain (for the moment) unchanged. The song of Rome, I think, represents in this last regard Browning's thrusting of the dream-poet Sordello away from Shelley's "unacknowledged legislator" role and towards a more Carlylean concern with action and the need to work at the work that is at hand. It is a test. History has its cruxes, and we have seen how Sordello handles his chance.

Browning's historicist outlook, which interrupts the narrator's first god-like call for the past to appear, will continue to bring the narrative to a halt, to circle it back upon itself with a motion that each time hands the "thread of discourse" (headnote to III, 1018-22 in 1863) over to the reader. But Browning's great dubiety finds the promise of an after-gust to be "over-bold." This word loops back through the end of Book III, where we are reminded to take our part in these terms:

> And having seen too what I saw, be bold
> Enough encounter what I do behold
> (That's sure) but you must take on trust! Attack
> The use and purpose of such sights! (III, 913-15)

And "over-bold" perfectly describes the hermeneutic sublime of the opening line, "Who will, may hear Sordello's story told," as well as the stance of a narrator who boldly brings his poetic lineage, "Fresh-chapleted to listen" (I, 25) into his poem. In Browning we find wary but necessary trust, not in history, but in the indispensable toil of the reader, even those disposed to "Attack" the work of the poet when compared with the work of the Salinguerras of the world. Browning's historicism is confrontational, and just as he does not "falter" when his Sordello is carved out of Dante's in order to be "'Gate-vein of this hearts' blood of Lombardy'" (I, 347), we must not falter in making Browning's Sordello our Sordello, including the character of the narrator. History is a song of the mighty chiefs of former years, but Browning makes sure we hear it as a difficult song, containing many unknown but crucial notes, grace notes as it were; we exert ourselves to hear its complex solidity, not its linear melody. In the next chapter we will look closely at the poetic techniques and strategies by which we hear Sordello's story told.

CHAPTER FOUR

The Techniques of Difficulty

I

Browning's *Sordello* is never entirely on the track: the poet/speaker presents himself as the master saboteur of his own narrative line. The local diversions and frequent anastrophic complications point to the artifice of the text and question the act of writing; like all such Shandyisms, they also become digressions into the question of reading. Any study of the structure of the poem must take into account the multiplicity and willfulness of Browning's derailments — not smooth over them. One of the best essays terms the digression which concludes Book III "amazingly illegitimate," a statement which reminds us of the relevance of the laws of genre.[1] In order for a digression to be considered lawful or unlawful the norms of the realm of the text must be understood, and for *Sordello*, textual "molestation" (to use a term of Edward Said's) becomes one of its laws. Thus the disjunctiveness and seeming incoherencies are stylistic reflections of Browning's poetics and of his ironic view of the world. Against this understanding of the difficulties of *Sordello*, we may juxtapose a traditional view, expounded most ably by William Clyde DeVane, which sees in the history of the revisions of the text an explanation for the seeming inconsistency of the poem's components and even the difficulties of its style; accordingly, the digression in Book III results because after reworking the "romantic love-element" in *Sordello* Browning "felt it necessary to apologize for diminishing its importance in the final version."[2] While this view is propped up by Browning's letter on the subject to Fanny Haworth, it is not supported by the text, which contains no apology (indeed, none would be necessary since no one had seen an earlier version replete with "romance"). Within the context of Browning's time, his stated aim to enforce reader "co-operation" in *Paracelsus*, and both friendly and hostile accounts of reading *Sordello*, it makes sense to regard its difficulties as rhetorical tactics which, while avoiding the easy projection of meaning determined by the author, might compel the reader to participate more fully. One of these tactics is surely that of Romantic irony (as Clyde de L. Ryals has ably demonstrated), and Browning's first decade of production coincides with the maturation of Carlyle as the foremost Romantic ironist in England. David Simpson has provided a concise definition:

> English Romantic irony, broadly put, consists in the studied avoidance on the artist's part of determinate meanings, even at such times as he might wish his reader to *produce* such meanings for himself; it involves the refusal of closure, the incorporation of any potentially available "metacomment" within the primary language of the text, the provision of a linguistic sign which moves towards or verges upon a "free" status, and the consequent raising to self-consciousness of the authoritarian element in discourse, and it affects both the author-reader relation and the intentional manipulation, from both sides, of the material through which they communicate.[3]

This statement describes *Sordello* aptly enough — but it sums up after-the-fact certain textual characteristics, rather than critical theories recognizable to writers whom we now view as practitioners of Romantic irony; the term "irony," in fact, is so rare in discourse about poetry before the 1840s that, while Schlegel is undoubtedly important, I am hesitant to use the phrase "Romantic irony" as though it described an aesthetic that would have been recognized by members of the literary community at that time. Given our current understanding of the traits called "Romantic Irony," Ryals is certainly right to call *Sordello* "one of the chief examples of Romantic irony in nineteenth-century English literature." But it might be argued that within the context of English literature, "Shandyism" has its own claim for defining these characteristics, as does "philosophic" or, since Browning predicts in Book III that in the future's estimation he will "Dance, forsooth, Metaphysic Poet" (829), "metaphysical."[4] However we define it, the key question remains that of intentionality: what aesthetics governs Browning's difficult style in *Sordello*? The idea that *Sordello* results from accident I think is a twentieth-century opinion boosted by the esteem that formalist critics held for the shorter monologues. Earlier critics often provide better clues to Browning's intent.

Though the tenor of most early commentary on *Sordello* was towards censure, most critics were aware that Browning had succeeded at what he set out to do. Lounsbury thought so, but he also found the goal to be morally reprehensible: "Never was there a more unblushing declaration on the part of an author of his willingness to shift upon the reader the burden of clearing a path through the jungle of his expression which he himself was too indolent or too indifferent to open up."[5] Edward

Dowden, a more friendly apologist, comes nearer the mark when he pictures the reader — not as a put-upon jungle hacker — but as an honest athlete: "When it needs a leaping-pole to pass from subject to verb across the chasm of a parenthesis, when the reader swings himself dubiously from relative to some one of three antecedents, and when these efforts are demanded again and again, some muscular fatigue naturally ensues."[6] As we have seen, "toil" is perhaps the key word for the reader in the 1830s, and to image the reading-act as Dowden does as a dubious Tarzan-swing over the abyss of meaning seems a post-modern apprehension of textual uniqueness, and points to the place of *Sordello* in the history of the modern long poem.

We may rephrase Dowden's image in terms familiar to modern phenomenology, particularly the works of Iser and Gadamer which rely on the concept of theme and horizon. In *Sordello* the various perspectives are interwoven in such a way that the theme is constantly in doubt for the reader; the ease with which narrative normally connects the theme of the moment to the horizon is deliberately frustrated by Browning in an attempt to make the reader survey several horizons simultaneously. The imposition of such a survey upon the reader may offer both ironic juxtapositions as well as sublime syntheses. (One of the critical tensions in the poem is between Sordello's aspirations towards the sublime and the narrator's ironic point of view.) Sterling's description of the act of reading *Sartor Resartus* gives us an idea of how a contemporary might view a work such as *Sordello*:

> Nothing beautiful here, nothing calmly, manifestly wise. We look at it not for its worth, but its oddity. Gradually the eye learns to find some dawning coherence and stability, as if it were not merely mist. Then one entanglement untwists itself after another: joint and lineament, plan and structure appear, intricate indeed, but palpable. At last we cross ourselves, and know not whether to laugh or weep, when we find that we were puzzled, not by the want of aught real and substantial in the object, but by the presence of so many more forms of truth and nature than we commonly discern in life, and which yet, although we knew them not, were ever there.[7]

Carlyle's compressive style results in a supra-abundance of meaning through the difficulties of its techniques; Browning's poem shares the aesthetic of *Sartor* and *The French Revolution*, and he expects to share the audience, too. In *Sordello* three of the techniques that make a doubled reading possible are self-referentiality, the structure of allusion, and the ongoing commentary on the act of writing *Sordello*, all of which run counter to the more normative horizons of plot sequentiality. In his excellent reading of the poem, Herbert F. Tucker focusses on the way in which "stuttering interruptions, checks, anticipations, and postponements give *Sordello* a stubbornly different meaning. They are its way of meaning."[8] This rhetoric of interruption, I believe, takes shape in allusiveness and paradiegesis (usually in the form of curious little narratives ostentatiously drawn from history's nooks, but read as parables). It is interesting to note that Browning's allusions rarely take us into the arena of literary influence; his use of parallel narratives, I think is an even more important study, since it is a technique that shapes *Sordello* and connects it to its companion poems *Paracelsus* and *Pippa Passes*.

II

By nature allusion calls for the reader's participation, since the reference is lost without the act of recognition. *Sordello* is an oddly allusive poem. It begins with an overt reference to *Don Quixote*, and brings immediately into the text the idea of an audience of fellow poets; it is a poem written for brothers, in a style which is self-consciously an example for them to follow; it is a style, however, which is so elliptical that, with a few exceptions, it prevents the pinpointing of direct reference to the texts of its audience of precursors. One of these allusions, the typological reference to Moses in the desert of "Zin the Horrid" (III, 816-29) is easily recognizable, but as Linda Peterson points out the allusion itself predicts the audience's reaction: "bewilderment, frustration, rebellion. What the audience wants is water — that is, the story of Sordello told in an intelligible manner."[9] Even in the case of Sordello's song of Rome, as we have seen, Browning compresses his treatment of Romantic precursors and relies on the reader's familiarity for effect. The way in which the reader may be expected to respond to oblique echoes, even with the "pointing pole" of such maieutic intrusions as "See you?" (I, 237), needs to be explored in order to determine the extent to which the phenomenon exists as a facet of the reader, and the extent it is directed by the text.

Modern study of literary influence (Bate, Bloom, et al.) stems from a recognition of the oblique allusiveness of Romantic poetry, as well as the anxious rhetoric of Romantic commentary on belatedness and the poetic tradition. The admixture of Freudian psychology with a view of canonicity that dehistoricizes poetic production produces a dark view of influence in which echoes are traces of deep psychic struggles. Whether such a theory is transhistorical and applicable to writers beyond the

Romantics is arguable in itself—despite Bloom's readings of "Childe Roland," many scholars find Browning relatively unanxious on the subject of Shelley. James K. Chandler, too, has recently noted how this school of thought begs the question of intentionality, and he points out how we often neglect to consider the *rhetoric* of allusion during the Romantic period, and the extent to which indirect allusions, which we may easily take as unconscious echoes, may in fact be intentional. Chandler usefully distinguishes Romantic practice from the more deliberate allusiveness of the early-eighteenth century, and notes how in the 1790s, as an outgrowth of the application of association psychology to criticism, the notion of unconscious allusiveness comes into play as a sign of the author's creativity.[10] Elizabeth Barrett discusses *Sordello* in terms of associative play when she writes to Browning:

An excellent solemn chiming, the passage from Dante makes with your Sordello and the Sordello *deserves* the labour which it needs, to make it appear the great work it is. I think that the principle of association is too subtly in movement throughout it—so that *while* you are going straight forward you go at the same time round & round, until the progress involved in the motion is lost sight of by the lookers on.

(*Letters of RB and EBB*, 1, p. 342)

It is thus feasible that, alongside the recombinative source-hunt of J. L. Lowes and the oedipal struggles of Bloom, we may read Romantic echoes (however oblique) as intentional acts, legitimate pieces of rhetoric based on the widespread belief in the powers of association. Browning's "chiming" with Dante is just one of the more obvious intertextual harmonies offered by Browning's poem.

Chandler has discussed the ways in which in Romantic lyrics the signals (or what Ziva Ben-Porat calls "markers") of allusion are muffled to the point that one cannot determine whether or not the reader is intended to recognize an allusion (whether the author intends to make one is another matter).[11] One of Browning's most curious forms of allusion may be categorized as the proleptic and portentous reference to poetry the reader cannot have read (yet): a later portion of *Sordello* itself. In *The New Spirit of the Age* (1844), Horne notes how the style of *Sordello* "abounds in things addressed to a second sight, and we are often required to *see double* in order to apprehend its meaning."[12] A description, for instance, or a visit by Salinguerra to Adelaide's chamber uses terms that the reader, at this early point in the poem, cannot possibly grasp:

> conceive; the orpine patch
> Blossoming earliest on our log-house-thatch
> The day those archers wound along the vines —
> Related to the Chief that left their lines
> To climb with clinking step the northern stair
> Up to the solitary chambers where
> Sordello never came.   (I, 657-63.)

Browning here not only slows down our reading, he forces a rereading by alluding to events which we will be able to unpuzzle only after we have finished the poem and started a second reading. But while these self-allusions are curious enough, I think more problematic is the insertion of brief authorial directions, such as the "conceive" in the passage above, which earlier I have termed "maieutic intrusions" because I think that they function in a Socratic way, acting as midwives to the reader's thought. These words seem to be markers for *possible* allusions, though exactitude of reference is rarely to be found; they may indicate intentional echoes, or spots in which each reader must search his or her associations to return or complete the echo. They certainly represent to us passages which the author signals as interpretive cruxes. Until recently few of these places have been explicated.[13]

Many crucial passages in *Sordello*, in fact, are frequently circumnavigated by critics who attempt to scout the coastline, discern the poem's major outlines, and then fit the terra incognita into their maps of Browning's career. One of the first such passages occurs about a fifth of the way into Book I, where, in an attempt to explain the essential and enduring nature of the historically dim conflict between the Guelfs and the Ghibellines, Browning resorts to a metaphorical description of the levelling of the upthrusting land by the sea. This tactically difficult passage concludes with one of the markers I have been discussing, in the form of a question: "See you?" (I, 237). This query to the reader (or narratees?) functions as an ironic demand for immediate re-reading, since few will have grasped much on initial perusal. It also alerts the reader to be aware of the complexity (and not the mere surface difficulty) of the image. An analysis of the language, coupled with an investigation of the metaphors of political position-taking in Browning's time, will help us to "see" what Browning is about. Browning's politics and the allusive tropes by which he connects his tale of Sordello to current events can be shown through a detailed explication, one that will also demonstrate the extreme compression of Browning's style. My own interpretation of this passage, then, may be taken as one reader's

sketching in the lines between the stars to form a constellation. But first it
will be useful to have the entire passage before us:

> Cliffs an earthquake suffered jut
> In the mid-sea, each domineering crest
> Nothing save such another throe can wrest
> From out (conceive) a certain chokeweed grown
> Since o'er the waters, twine and tangle thrown
> Too thick, too fast accumulating round,
> Too sure to over-riot and confound
> Ere long each brilliant islet with itself
> Unless a second shock save shoal and shelf,
> Whirling the sea-drift wide: alas, the bruised
> And sullen wreck! Sunlight to be diffused
> For that! Sunlight, 'neath which, a scum at first,
> The million fibres of our chokeweed nurst
> Dispread themselves, mantling the troubled main,
> And, shattered by those rocks, took hold again
> So kindly blazed it — that same blaze to brood
> O'er every cluster of the multitude
> Still hazarding new clasps, ties, filaments,
> An emulous exchange of pulses, vents
> Of nature into nature; till some growth
> Unfancied yet exuberantly clothe
> A surface solid now, continuous, one:
> The Pope, for us the People, who begun
> The People, carries on the People thus,
> To keep that Kaiser off and dwell with us!
> See you?   (I, 213-37)

Browning's political sympathies in *Sordello* (when they are considered
important at all to the "development of a soul") are usually considered
to lie with "the people." While Alan Chaffee in a recent essay consistently depoliticizes Browning's many uses of "people" and "crowd" in order
to see as the basis of the poem a dialectic between the self and the other,
Browning's use of these terms is politically charged.[14] In a letter to
Fanny Haworth (May, 1840), he declares his sympathy in *Sordello* for
"Mankind,the while poor-devildom one sees cuffed and huffed from
morn to midnight" (*New Letters*, p. 18). DeVane roundly declares that
after Browning's trip to Italy in 1838 "henceforth he was a Liberal, a
champion of the cause of the people in England, France, or Italy."[15]
And Mrs. Sutherland Orr, looking back from the triumphant Liberalism
of the end of the century, summarizes the political leanings of the first

103

book by a paraphrase of the passage above; she maintains that the theme is the struggle of the Ghibellines and the Guelfs, "the one symbolized by isolated heights, the other by continuous level growth; those again suggesting the violent disruptions which create imperial power; these the peaceful organic processes of democratic life."[16] This paraphrase, though, is an illegitimate deduction from a passage which vouchsafes no clear-cut interpretation; at the very least, the happy connotations of "continuous level growth" are not authorized by such words as "chokeweed" and "scum." And the "friendless people," after all, are befriended only by Don Quixote, who sees as people what are in reality stampeding sheep.

In addition, the passage contains significant ambiguities which deflect us from linear reading. For instance, the cliffs are presented as an "earthquake suffered jut / In the mid-sea." Does this mean cliffs "that" an earthquake suffered "to" jut, or is "jut" a noun? "Crest" is next applied not to the waves, but to the cliffs, implying a kind of geologic wave action. The parenthetical use of "(conceive)" — does this direct the reader to produce his or her own image? These relatively minor difficulties are compounded by the problems of identifying the speaker. In the first edition, *Sordello* often suggests a welter of voices, a cacophony from the past. Browning's addition of quotation marks in his revision of 1863, however, gives the reader a sense of false security; it is all-too-easy to assume that everything *not* in quotation marks is thus voiced by the narrator. But here the puzzling particularity of a "certain" chokeweed, "our" chokeweed, when aligned with the lines immediately preceding the passage quoted above, makes it plausible that, although Browning later placed quotation marks only around lines 234-36, we are hearing a voice other than (or doubled with) the narrator's throughout. These lines are clearly spoken by someone with a personal stake in the conflict — how else do we explain the point of view of "crowd of feudatories... That leapt down... to our fields"? (206-08); in 1863, however, Browning did not choose to place quotation marks around these lines, possibly indicating half a "voice," a point in which the discourse of the past creeps into the narratorial flow. It is a voice which in the dramatic context merges into the narrator's creative act.

While the problem of voice extends throughout *Sordello*, a number of individual words in this passage call attention to themselves. The use of the word "chokeweed" is especially curious; it commonly refers not to seaweed, but to a parasitic land plant. This "chokeweed" would seem to represent the people, a rather Carlylean multitude which has yet to learn how to recognize and defer to the god-sent hero. A second shock is needed to stave off the confounding of "each brilliant islet with itself" (another ambiguity: "itself" plausibly refers to both "chokeweed" and "islet" — here we have one of those "dubious swings" of which Dowden spoke), and this phrase introduces an enigmatic exclamation to end the thicket of syntax: "alas, the bruised / And sullen wreck!"

"Wreck" would seem to refer to the chokeweed, which has been whirled about, but could equally apply to the cliffs; as rhetoric, the expression works as a kind of skewed epiphonema, personified by "bruised and sullen" far beyond the demands of the descriptive mode. The transformation of the chokeweed into a wreck, however, turns Browning's trope towards a more favorable treatment of the seaweed; it emerges from the exchange as a reticulative organism with an "emulous exchange of pulses, vents / Of nature into nature." This growth "unfancied yet" is clearly evolutionary, and evokes the organic image which is the standard Romantic metaphor for a work of art. Browning's figure now may represent Mrs. Orr's "peaceful organic processes," except that the political stance seems less pro-liberal, and more bipartisan or dialectical. The "people" are presented as weeds and scum and wreck, which, out of confrontation with the cliffs, will become something more. In Book V, when Sordello pours out his soul to Salinguerra in the people's behalf, it is "for that age, a novel thing" (V, 455), the result of the processes of history in which, through the unselfish efforts of individuals, old things are transcended:

> 'Tis knowledge, whither such perceptions tend:
> They lose themselves in that, means to an end,
> The Many Old producing some One New,
> A Last unlike the First. (V, 443-46)

This recognition of the gradual nature of change marks the age's defense of hope against the cynicism inspired by the failure of the previous era's revolutionary fervor. One of the points of congruence between Browning and Shelley, despite Shelley's seeming millenarianism, is in the perception of progress in unpromising phenomena, and Browning's nautical imagery may remind us of the preface to *The Revolt of Islam*, in which Shelley muses on the relationship of his poem to the French Revolution, noting that "there is a reflux in the tide of human things which bears the shipwrecked hopes of men into a secure haven after the storms are past," and he concludes that "I am aware, methinks, of a slow, gradual, silent change."[17] Carlyle provides another point of

105

reference; twenty or so years after Shelley's poem he uses the characteristic image of the wreck not so much for failed hopes as for the collapse of both the utopian dream and the pre-revolutionary status-quo:

> For myself, in these days, I seem to see in this indestructibility of hero-worship the ever-lasting adamant lower than which the confused wreck of revolutionary things cannot fall. The confused wreck of things crumbling and even crashing and tumbling all round us in these revolutionary ages, will get down so far; no farther. (*Works*, 5:15)

Carlyle's ideas in his "heroism" lectures were common coin in his intellectual circle in the 1830s. The play of the hero against the sea/ground of the masses is fully integrated into the structure of metaphor in *The French Revolution*: "The cry, *To arms*, roars tenfold; steeples with their metal storm-voice boom out, as the sun sinks; armorers' shops are broken open, plundered; the streets are a living foam-sea, chafed by all the winds" (*Works*, 2, p. 177). One critic notes how in the book "the mob is an organism, a 'Life-Sea', and its movements follow a life cycle like that of a plant."[18] In Book III, Browning describes a crowd beneath a balcony in terms which remind us of Carlyle's dramatic, present-tense recounting of the Revolution:

> A balcony lay black beneath until
> Out 'mid a gush of torchfire grey-haired men
> Came on it and harangued the people: then
> Sea-like that people surging to and fro
> Shouted, Hale forth the Carroch.... (III, 286-90)

The images of sea and wreck, which serve Shelley as well as Carlyle for revolutionary effects (whether of the 1790s or the 1830s), are clearly not fortuitous in Browning's passage; this oddly "bruised and sullen wreck" certainly carries contemporary reference to the "wreck of revolutionary things" — both Shelleyan hopes, and Carlylean tearing down of old order. The life sea represents, of course, the promise (or threat) of the leveling of property, the erosion of traditional values, the loss of the things, like the cliffs of Dover, that symbolize England. One of Horne's early works provides these lines:

> ... the spirit of changed,
> And love of liberty, are now abroad,
> Which, if not stopped, will, like a sweeping flood
> Poured over vineyards, gardens, parks, and meads,
> Reduce all property to a level surface.[19]

106

Within this metaphoric field, Browning's originality is in his use of the key word, "wreck": by forsaking the paradigm of the *ship*-wreck so prevalent in Romantic iconography, and applying instead the word's revolutionary reference to the more impersonal biological/geological metaphor of the seaweed/cliffs, Browning implies both the evolutionary, natural process of historical change, and comments on another topical image for revolution: the deluge.[20]

Quite naturally, considering the narrator's extraordinary gesture of banishing Shelley's shade from his presence before beginning his tale, Shelley is the precursor whom critics consider first in *Sordello*; in fact, Shelley's "baleful influence" has become as much a distraction in studies of the early Browning as Mill's comments on *Pauline*.[21] But Lord Byron, unbanished, provides the most interesting analogue for our passage. He is the Napoleon of literature, a poet whom the adolescent Browning (along with the rest of his generation) deeply admired.[22] More importantly, Byron was a poet, like Sordello, who was torn between poetry and political action, but who ultimately chose the latter. In effect, the efficacy of Byron's death at Missolonghi is one of the subterranean concerns of *Sordello*. Closer to the point, Byron was also famously involved in the struggle for Italian liberty; John Galt in 1830 interprets *Sardanapalus* as an "insight of the cogitations of the poet, whether to take part in the hazardous activity which they [the carbonari] were preparing."[23] In a journal entry of 1821 (published by Moore in 1830, when Browning was eighteen, in the bestselling *Life*), Byron describes his ambivalent feelings about a possible insurrection in terms which suggest Browning's metaphor of water, seaweed, and jutting and eroding cliffs:

> They mean to insurrect here, and are to honour me with a call thereupon. I shall not fall back; though I don't think them in force or heart sufficient to make much of it. But, *onward!* — it is now time to act, and what signifies *self*, if a single spark of that which would be worthy of the past can be bequeathed unquenchedly to the future? It is not one man, nor a million, but the *spirit* of liberty which must be spread. The waves which dash upon the shore are, one by one, broken, but yet the *ocean* conquers, nevertheless. It overwhelms the Armada, it wears the rock, and, if the *Neptunians* are to be believed, it has not only destroyed, but made a world. In like manner, whatever the sacrifice of individuals the great cause will gather strength, sweep down what is rugged, and fertilize (for *sea-weed* is *manure*) what is cultivable.[24]

One of the aims of criticism is to discover the issues that control the choices that a writer makes. While Browning's passage would not be recognizable as an "allusion" to Byron, in the formal sense of allusion as a reference that is meant to be recognized by every cultivated reader, Byron's recognition in his journal of the necessity of *action* (even at the risk of the obliteration of the individual) is not irrelevant to *Sordello*.

Byron, a domineering jut of a poet, debates the necessity of mingling with the waves and sea-weed to fertilize the future, to transmit the one spark that will signify. Sordello is confronted in the end with a similar choice. In Book VI he imagines the possible future of "the people," but also realizes how little one man can do to bring it about:

> Down sank the People's Then; uprose their Now.
> These sad ones render service to! And how
> Piteously little must that service prove
> —Had surely proved in any case!   (VI, 159-62)

The "piteous little" is an intimation of a failing of the second class of poet: enervation from a realization of the inability of the will to exercise itself to effect change. And the service, no matter how little, entails some loss of individuality; Browning here keenly feels the paradox which is implicit in Byron's journal entry — the individual fame of the poet which makes his service (potentially) worth rendering will be swallowed up by the sea. In Sordello's thoughts, again: "Read the black writing — that collective man / Outstrips the individual!" (V, 103-04). Salinguerra, Browning's Carlylean hero, instead moves with the tide, and accepts mingling as a condition of doing. He declares in Book IV:

> Another life's ordained me: the world's tide
> Rolls, and what hope of parting from the press
> Of waves, a single wave through weariness
> That's gently led aside, laid upon shore?   (IV, 811-14)

Now according to Mrs. Orr and DeVane, Salinguerra should be a "cliff" and not part of the sea, whose waters may indeed be getting metaphorically murky. But, if we may set that interpretation aside for a moment, I would like to persevere with a few more observations on the contexts of Browning's metaphors, and especially his choice of the word "People," and his emphasis on it throughout the poem.

For the poet in the Romantic era, the "people" thus phrased means more than the sum total of the human beings within national boundaries. Sordello in Book VI must choose how to "render service" to these people, and his failure at this crossroads leaves the task (grown more difficult) to Dante. These people "Then" and "Now" represent different audiences; as visionary judges which gather for Sordello when he makes his great pitch to Salinguerra, they symbolize the poet's audience as it extends through time, and they parallel the conjured audience whom the narrator addresses at the opening of the poem. This concept is an acceptable political authorization for the otherwise elitist "fit audience" paradigm, and we have seen how Shelley formulates it in just such a manner.[25] Sordello of course fails this audience, but the correctness of his belated attempt is reinforced by his position as Dante's forerunner. In plucking the obscure Sordello from Dante's text, Browning shadows the importance of the later poet as a model for a successful poetic *action* (Sordello himself represents a current 1830s impasse). Sordello's successors — Dante, Petrarch, Tasso — were widely considered as epitomes of the poet-as-creator and also as models of political and social efficacy. In an early commentary on Dante (1830), Bulwer contrasts the trans-historical "people" with the "Time" (i.e., the reading "Public"):

> I make this distinction between Time and the People — for the Time has a short life and the People a long one. It rarely happens that the most popular writer for the time is the writer most preserved by the people. . . . It is only in the very rare instances, such as Petrarch and Dante, that the taste of the time unites with the judgment of the generations that form a people as to the rank which a nation accords to its poet.[26]

And Petrarch furnishes to Leigh Hunt the example of just how much a poet, through the action of the pen, might do:

> One love, and one poet, sufficed to give the whole civilized world a sense of delicacy in desire, of the abundant riches to be found in one single idea, and of the going out of man's self to dwell in the soul and happiness of another, which has served to refine the passion for all modern times.[27]

Sordello's early flaw, placed within this context, becomes more explicable, for it is defined in similar terms: "That is, he loves not, nor possesses One / Idea that, star-like over, lures him on / To its exclusive purpose" (II, 395-97); it is in lines like these, in their tangential relation to the "idea" of Petrarch, that Browning's audience of poets haunts his pages. Sordello does eventually discover his single idea in his understanding of his oneness with the people. As he lectures Salinguerra: "Already you include / The multitude; now let the multitude / Include yourself, and the result is new" (V, 533-35). Before this point, however, the narrator puts a question directly to Sordello, and parenthetically connects the problem to the contemporary English scene: "Were you

109

the first who got, to use plain speech, / The Multitude to be materialized?" (V, 124-25). (In 1867 Browning made the point more explicit by changing "plain speech" to "modern speech.") But Sordello never has the impact of a Petrarch or a Dante, because he fails to take "the one step too mean / For him to take" (VI, 830-31). We may place this failure now within the terms of the early passage which sparked the discussion; for Sordello and his age the multitudinous sea of people (the chokeweed and scum, from one perspective) fail to be catalyzed into the growth unfancied yet.[28]

Browning's metaphoric definition of the Ghibellines and Guelfs, then, alludes outward to the political attitudes of Browning's England, as well as alerting us to the supercharged use of such a common word as "people." Browning's trope exploits the metaphorical "field" of his time, causing a paratactic reverberation in the process of reading. Thomas McFarland, in a recent essay that posits the "anteriority of field" in literature, describes five patterns of the Zeitgeist which shape the work of art. The final one is "Aphycton," which "exists when the inner logic of an intellectual emphasis leads to a similar disposition of metaphorical materials even when no influence is present."[29] Browning's pattern of diction throughout *Sordello* displays a canny awareness of the workings of this "inner logic." In the 1830s, people (i.e., the "Public") were acutely aware of the leveling motion of revolutionary activity, a fear carried over from the French wars which was succinctly expressed in 1813 by one of Napoleon's foes, Benjamin Constant: "Human beings are sacrificed to abstractions: a holocaust of individuals is offered up to 'the people.'"[30] This fear did not die with the defeat of Napoleon, and made a natural resurgence in the 1830s, when reform agitation and the enfranchisement of some of the middle-class threatened to level the distinctions of the British social structure; when the narrator interjects in Book VI, "Oh, People, urge / Your claims!" (143-44) he speaks directly to the reader of 1840. As with the earlier period of tumult during the French wars (though one must recognize that the entire era was full of unrest), one of the most persistent images in literature and art is that of inundation. Browning's description of the Guelf / Ghibelline conflict also must be read against the background of a flourishing subgenre — the Cuvierian representation of catastrophic floods.

"Roll on, thou deep and dark blue Ocean — roll!" Byron's words are echoed in the numerous paintings and poems on the subject of the deluge which (no matter how doggedly biblical) also comment oblique-ly on the political metaphor — Carlyle's "Life-Sea." The exhibitions at

110

the Royal Academy and British Institution rarely failed to display a "deluge" painting, and Turner and his rivals John Martin and Francis Danby all painted large canvases (Martin's was widely disseminated in his own mezzotint version of 1828). There were in the 1830s at least four book-length poems on the subject of the flood.[31] The painting that most clearly reveals the relevancy of this genre to Browning's passage is Danby's monumental *Deluge* painted in 1837-1840 and exhibited in London in the latter year. This canvas features a high jutting cliff in the left center, surrounded by tumultuous waters filled with multitudes of human forms, some of whom vainly attempt to climb the cliff to safety.[32] Danby's "sea-drift" is not chokeweed, but drowning humanity; the people are sympathized with, but not offered hope. Despite the striking visual parallel, Browning's image is more hopeful than Danby's (and other deluge paintings) because he agrees with Byron's Neptunians, that the waters have "not only destroyed, but made a world." Through the language of metaphor, Browning speaks to the problems of the radicalism of "the people," and to the necessity of liberal change. Browning's trope of the cliffs and the sea describes the Guelf/Ghibelline conflict, and indirectly comments on the fear of political deluge. Implicit in the figure, too, is the recognition that, as Byron realized, when the moment comes some individual sacrifice must be made in order to "transmit the spark." To borrow a contemporaneous coinage of De Quincey's, this passage, (along with much of *Sordello*) works through a kind of allusive "introvolution." The figure of speech, ostensibly used to illuminate the differences between two Italian factions, whirls inward through the reverberations of language, until it connects with contemporary writing and the debate on the subject of "the people." Both destructive and progressive change are inevitable; the reader who follows directions — "See you?" — may be treated to the imaginative sight of the gradual appearance of the "growth unfancied yet" which marks Browning's own post-diluvian hopes.

III

The analysis of this quasi-allusive passage, with its concluding (though hardly conclusive) "See you?", I hope demonstrates one of the ways Browning disrupts his story to force the reader's "co-operating fancy" to frame to a constellation of meaning for himself. Browning in his post-*Sordello* period resorts to the theory of the drama (via of course the dramatic monologue) to enforce this co-operation. He says in a letter to

Elizabeth Barrett (10 August, 1845), which fusses at the "easy work" which novelists have, that the "Dramatic poet" represents speech-actions directly and so puts it "in *your* power, to *name*, characterize and so raise or blame, *what* is so said and done... if you don't perceive of yourself there is no standing by, for the Author, and telling you" (*Letters of RB and EBB*, 1, p. 150). Now in *Sordello* the speaker does stand by, "pointing pole" in hand, to help us with the "unexampled themes"; but these themes are not delivered to the reader in the manner of a novelist (or poets who tell novels in verse), but are instead intimated through little stories within the narrative proper, apocro-allusive passages, and the play of voices which asks us to fill up the interstices between interruptions. One brief example occurs in Book III:

> if the true diadem
> Seemed imminent while our Sordello drank
> The wisdom of that golden Palma, thank
> Verona's Lady in her Citadel
> Founded by the Gaulish Brennus legends tell —
> And truly when she left him the sun reared
> A head like the first clamberer's that peered
> A-top the Capitol, his face on flame
> With triumph, triumphing till Manlius came.   (III, 584-92)

The commonplace metaphor of drinking wisdom leads to the idea of thanking a statue of the Madonna centered (we learn from modern annotations) in a fountain; the statue is associated with its citadel, and its founder Brennus — and then in an extraordinary leap, even for *Sordello*, Palma's exit provokes (truly!) a simile in which the sun is compared with the face of the first man to climb atop the Capitol during Brennus' attack (c. 390) on Rome. Manlius kills this man — and the completion of the sequence of tropes is that Sordello's grasp of the "true diadem" (the "proper service" — III, 581 — of the people) will be as fleeting as the first climber's view of Rome. It is another compressed and highly ironic version, in fact, of the dream vision of Rome in the next Book.

As another example, I would like to take an in-depth look at the section in Book I in which the subject of "Apollo" is introduced. Browning's discussion develops as an addendum to a seemingly disinterested bifurcation of poets into two classes. In this analysis of poets, the terms are bounded by the subjective / objective dichotomy that was commonplace in the 1830s. As Bulwer says in one of his first periodical pieces:

We hear a great deal about the difference between the Objective and the Subjective order of Genius — i.e., between the writer who casts himself out among others and so forgets his individuality, and the writer who subjects others to himself, and in treating of them still preserves his individuality.[33]

Browning's narrator leaves us to guess at the jargon, but the categories of his two classes are clearly similar, and his extensive use of the terms in the "Essay on Shelley" (1851) dates from an acquaintance with subjective/objective dualities made in his early years as a poet. He begins with a detailed description of Sordello as a boy "foremost in the regal class / Nature has broadly severed from her mass" (I, 467-68). These poets "are fain invest / The lifeless thing with life from their own soul" (I, 490-91), but, because "they would belong / To what they worship" (I, 509-10) they eventually become slaves to their own creations. This is Browning's rather Blakean exegesis of the way in which poets hypostatize their own personifications (or myths) and thus found religions. (Something similar occurs in the complicated metamorphosis of the "young witch" passage in *Pauline*.) The descriptive pretext is next abandoned (Sordello and Goito are left in the background) and a second class of poets is introduced, one which "proclaims each new revealment born a twin / With a distinctest consciousness within" (I, 525-26). This class the narrator now suggests may be part of an evolutionary vanguard, for, after a passage in which such a poet voices his own claim, the narrator defines the poet as a pioneer, what Ezra Pound would later call the "antennae of the race":

> In truth? Thou hast
> Life, then — wilt challenge life for us: thy race
> Is vindicated so, obtains its place
> In thy ascent, the first of us; whom we
> May follow, to the meanest, finally,
> With our more bounded wills? (I, 548-53)

This question, posed in terms which suggest the narrator's sarcastic view of any who claim "unbounded wills," is immediately followed by a delineation of two pitfalls which await such a strong-willed pioneer. Sordello falls into both enervation, caused by the realization that the world is "Too narrow an arena" (I, 558), and the desire for an absolute mastery in this world, which should properly be reserved for the next.

Browning sees the second, more Napoleonic flaw, as the most detrimental; these poets desire "to put all / That nature forth" and thus thrust "in time eternity's concern" (I, 562-66). This desire begins from the false premise that the poet is a god, and it has dire consequences: heaven alone is for perfection, and mortals who attempt to draw perfection down to earth, to make hearth-fire out of the divine spark, will pay a price. The penalty is figured as a plague, "the mark / Of leprosy" (I, 567-68), but Browning's trope twists the center of gravity from the tenor to the vehicle, or signifier. At first this image seems to leap from nowhere, but it does connect, first perhaps as an allusion to the passage in *Paracelsus* in which the hero tells Festus that his curse is "A plague fit: you are not a lazar-haunter, / How should you know?" (III, 759-60; in 1849 Browning connects the passages more tightly by changing "A plague fit" to "The plague's sign," which corresponds to "mark"). It also prepares the ground for the introduction of Apollo, since to compete with the god is to invite the use of his plague-arrows. Apollo is introduced for the first time through a story which, by a series of substitutions, emerges from this idea of the plague "mark," and serves as a parabolic conclusion to the topic. In the age of Marcus Aurelius a Roman army sacks Babylon, and "in rummaging the rarities" of the temple of Apollo some soldiers greedily open a coffer, and let loose the "plague" (I, 595). Apollo is thus first associated with the pest, which is personified in graphically unpleasant terms as a "hag" with "blotchy bosom thick in spot" (I, 599-600). It is with this tale fresh in mind, and with the plague trope still turning our attention to the nature of metaphor itself, that the narrator returns us to a portrait of the artist as a young Apollo.

Sordello's arrival at the stage in which he fancies himself Apollo is handled facetiously by the speaker. Sordello's use of metonymy is a primitive case of metaphoric visualization; the name "Apollo" stands in for the fancied grandeur of the boy's power, exemplifying a kind of "deviance of denomination," to use a term of Paul Ricoeur's. Sordello's simple figure is skewered by the narrator's much more sophisticated use of metaphor, one that is based in the twisting deviance of the predicate.[34] The narrator uses images of motley and theft, and references to the antique and the act of discovery, to harken the reader back to the story of the sack of Apollo's Shrine:

> Wherefore twist and torture this,
> Striving to name afresh the antique bliss,
> Instead of saying, neither less nor more,
> He had discovered, as our world before,
> Apollo? That shall be the name; nor bid
> Me rag by rag expose how patchwork hid

> The man — what thefts of every clime and day
> Contributed to purfle the array
> He climbs with (June's at deep) some close ravine.   (I, 893-901)

The Apollo motif is thus shadowed by the irony of its origin in transgression and plague; at each iteration we sense the "hag" (the visual and sexual opposite of the young god) biding her time. Even the seemingly pro forma comparison of Palma and Daphne has its secret plague mark. For Apollo, Daphne becomes the laurel which is awarded to poets, or victors in games; the palm is the symbol of martial conquest, and Palma (known to Dante as Cunizza — Browning's name change is not innocent) wishes to take Sordello to Salinguerra (whom she alone recognizes as "Apollo's" sire) so he might be transformed into a palm-winning warrior (see III, 545-51).

Browning's highly idiosyncratic and quasi-allusive style is used here to make a potentially simple point (men should not try to be gods) very complex, and the issue is transformed into a multi-faceted critique of aspiration, with implications reaching into the question of authority in writing and reading. The play of voices in this section is particularly interesting; there are suggestive fissures between one speaker and the next, which often seem to slide about on successive readings. For instance, in the discussion of poetic flaws, the ellipsis is highly problematic:

> or if yet worse befall,
> And a desire possess it to put all
> That nature forth, forcing our straitened sphere
> Contain it; to display completely here
> The mastery another life should learn,
> Thrusting in time eternity's concern,
> So that Sordello... Fool, who spied the mark
> Of leprosy upon him, violet dark
> Already as he loiters?   (I, 561-69)

What I would like to argue about the use of aposiopesis in the lines above is that it signals an implicit dialogue, and it helps us to see how we should be reacting to the poem. Though it is impertinent to second-guess Browning's placement of quotation marks in 1863 (which distinguish a speaker in lines 558-61, but not in the lines above),[35] I suspect that the analysis of the second class's desire to thrust in time eternity's concern is offered by one of the narratees in answer to the narrator's question (line 553). This speaker leaps too quickly and with too much authority for the narrator's comfort to the case of Sordello; the narrator thus interrupts to ask, "Fool, who spied the mark . . . ?"

The phrase "So that Sordello . . ." begins an ur-narrative which is molested by the narrator at the point of adumbration; it is a sample of one narratee beginning to concretize (and thus over-determine) his expectations of where the narrative is heading. The reader here senses the "pointing pole" not of the narrator (who resents having something proleptically pointed out) but of the author who now traces by dramatic example the rules of a kind of game between narrator and narratee (author and reader). Complicating this notion is the further character- ization of the narrator as a cranky autocrat ("Fool," he says impatiently). The narrator's changing tones, as well as the play of other voices, reminds us of *Tristram Shandy*, though Browning's elisions are not signaled and reversed as clearly as Sterne's, and they usually indicate more than one motif. They are gaps with many possible bridges. One indication here is that we should both complete the thought begun by our surrogate, the narratee, as well as be wary of seeing this flaw (of monstrous, Napoleonic will) as the master-key to the story. Browning it would seem has brought us to the borders of an abyss in which should we drop off we may (if we will) soar above in an atmosphere of free interpretation.

The theme of Herbert F. Tucker's analysis of *Sordello*, in fact, is the way in which Browning skirts the problem of closure, as symbolized by Eglamor, who paradoxically, "ever initiates a fresh pursuit. Here [VI, 797-819, when Eglamor returns] Browning discovers the groundless play he has been seeking and discovers it in the strangest way imaginable: in the regenerative entrance of his own spirit of closure."[36] The spirit of play is certainly a key concept, but "groundlessness" is not an adequate description; rather it is the play of the contextual grounds against one another that provides the liberty. The spirit of Napoleon (and Byron, the Napoleon of rhyme), for instance, is the ground against which Browning reworks the Faust (or limitless quest of the Will) motif in his early works. As Dowden long ago noted of *Paracelsus* and *Sordello*: "'Je sens en moi l'infini,' exclaimed Napoleon one day, with his hand upon his breast. 'Je sens en moi l'infini' is the germ-idea of these poems."[37] It is an idea that is recapitulated and ironized in many ways, but always with a concern for the reader who is struggling to, at the very least, free himself from the toils of the text; we are made aware that the Imperial fiat by which the text may be closed (or scoffed at, or reviewed) is not a valid option.

116

Indeterminacy in the development of the Apollo motif is further reinforced by the way in which the narrator completes the thought, using imagery which metaleptically careens through plague and pest tropes until we are offered that most readerly-active of genres, the parable; as Browning puts it when introducing another such tale in Book III, "Ponder a story ancient pens transmit" (III, 989):

> Go back to the beginning rather; blend
> It gently with Sordello's life; the end
> Is piteous, you shall see, but much between
> Pleasant enough; meantime some pyx to screen
> The full-grown pest, some lid to shut upon
> The Goblin! As they found at Babylon,
> (Colleagues mad Lucious and sage Antonine)
> Sacking the city, by Apollo's shrine
> Its pride, — rummaging the rarities,
> A cabinet; be sure, who made the prize
> Opened it greedily; and out there curled
> Just such another plague, for half the world
> Was stung. Crawl in then, hag, and crouch asquat,
> Keeping that blotchy bosom thick in spot
> Until your time is ripe! The coffer-lid
> Is fastened and the coffer safely hid
> Under the Loxian's choicest gifts of gold.
> Who will may hear Sordello's story told.   (I, 587-604)

The fault perceived by the narratee is interpreted metaphorically by the narrator as a mark of leprosy, which is personified as a Goblin, and then the Goblin is interpreted through this allusion to an obscure story from the yet deeper past. Browning's use of parables, riddle-like allusive narratives for the most part, is always in *Sordello* an overture for reader response, and Browning reinforces a notion of the reader's power at this stage by rounding off this parallel narrative (as he does also in Book III) with a repetition of the opening line, "Who will may hear Sordello's story told."

His story? What have we been told here? — not to anticipate, not to jump to the conclusion, because piteous though it be it cannot be encompassed by the logic of "so that." The instructions at this point are to defer to the "meantime," and the pestilent imagery takes on dual referents. It of course first refers to the mark spied on Sordello, this desire for an omnipotent, god-like will. But it also refers to a parallel hubris on the part of the reader, to come to some one meaning and void the

117

processional, time-bound concerns of the text as it exists in the interplay between writer and reader. It is reading the brotherly love of the poem through the "Law." The "pyx to screen / The full-grown pest" is found in Browning's use of paradiegesis to force the reader into slower, more imaginative reading, and to keep him from rampaging through the story looking for the coffer that contains a singular "meaning." It is an equivalent to the famous "Macready pause," which contemporary reviewers charged Browning with catering to in *Strafford*.[38] Browning's tropes hint at an end, but in such a way that they ask us not to dwell on it: "Go back to the beginning, rather, blend / It gently...." Tucker describes the story told about John of Patmos that ends Book III as a "parable of interpretation" in which "the point" is Browning's rigorous demand for attention to the act of reading.[39] This earlier story, coming as it does after an interdicted ending begun "So that Sordello..." is perhaps a more severe, though more oblique, warning to the reader. The *reader* (as well as the poet) may attempt to be god-like. By implication, "Apollo" is thus not the goal of Sordello, but the ambition we all must beware, since lying under these golden gifts is this curiously overdescribed "hag" biding her (narrative) time.

IV

In *Tristram Shandy*, Sterne makes an offhand declaration about the play of thought between writer and reader that is a good starting point for a few final comments about the act of reading necessitated by Browning's techniques of difficulty in *Sordello*:

> Writing, when properly managed, (as you may be sure I think mine is) is but a different name for conversation: As no one, who knows what he is about in good company, would venture to talk all; — so no author, who understands the just bounds of decorum and good breeding, would presume to think all.[40]

Sterne ironically finds good manners in a mode of writing which many readers felt to be perplexing and rude; Browning manages, through his narrator's fluctuating discourse, to exceed decorum's boundaries, to molest the flow of narrative and generic expectations, and thus to rouse the reader into thought. In an age in which the public preferred (to quote again from *Philip van Artevelde*), lays "that shall not trouble thee to

118

think," Browning steers his long poem in a diametrically opposite course. When he later veers back around towards less difficult tactics, during his middle period, Browning finds a larger readership, but never apologizes for his much-maligned *Sordello*. His attitude towards his tactics of difficulty and his reception remains constant, as he declares to Domett in 1846: "I never was much disturbed in my natural post of 'most unintelligible of writers,' nor, consequently, got a tithe of the notice book-makers get as a matter of course — yet my gettings, what all the unintelligibility and unpopularity in the world could not preserve me from gettings — quite enough has been, indeed!" (*RB & AD*, p. 125). In the letter to Field (previous quoted) in 1855, Browning adamantly declares about *Sordello* that "the good of it is to be got at even now by the pains-taking," and in a later epistle to W. G. Kingslake he defends his "difficulty" by referring to the "fit audience" idea of his youth:

> ... I never designedly tried to puzzle people, as some of my critics have supposed. On the other hand, I never pretended to offer such literature as should substitute for a cigar, or a game of dominoes, to an idle man. So perhaps, on the whole, I got my desserts and something over, — not a crowd, but a few I could value more. (*Letters*, pp. 128-29)

The members of this "fit audience, though few," through their participation in the poem's dialogues, are lured into a conversation that in effect makes them "poets." Browning's call for brother's speech is an ideal version of what the reader, presuming he or she is properly toiling away, is experiencing in part. While Daniel Stempel thinks that this description is intended literally only for practicing fellow poets, it is clear, I believe, that Browning addresses the poet in us all.[41] His attempt at improved communication, however, is not naive; while some critics feel that at this stage of his career Browning "like Sordello and the speaker ... wanted to be all inclusive" and omnipotent,[42] it is clear that *Sordello* displays at all levels a keen awareness of human limitations, especially a knowledge that language is "the vehicle / Never sufficient" (V, 653-54).

One way of reminding us of the limitations of language is through the vacillating attitude of the narrator towards his poet-subject and the potentialities of art itself; in a verse paragraph towards the end of the third book, the narrator questions: "Attack / The use and purpose of such sights?" (III, 915-16). He argues for the Salinguerras of the world, but his deflation of transcendentalism turns to asking "where's the hurt / To keep the Makers-see on the alert" (III, 927-28) and concludes by boasting of his creative power to the conjured audience:

> And therefore have I moulded, made anew
> A Man, delivered to be turned and tried,
> Be angry with or pleased at. On your side
> Have ye times, places, actors of your own?
> Try them upon Sordello once full-grown,
> And then — ah then!   (III, 934-39)

Browning's figure here of the poem-as-man reaches to the heart of metaphor, and demands that in order to read we make our own tropes, twisting, turning, trying our imaginations against his text. To be a "makers-see" is to be a metaphor maker; the reader confronts the indeterminacies in this very passage, and ultimately must stand by his own imaginative construction. What Iser calls "negations" — the thwarting of generic expectations, for example — exist on a broad level within the poem's critique of reading itself. Browning's poem substantially denies our expectation that when the poem makes a turn, the reader will quickly connect similitudes and be back on a familiar road.

In *Sordello*, Browning explores the possibility of turning the epical long poem's potential for endlessness free. The completion (if this word isn't too inappropriate) of this early step may be found in the involutions of modern epical texts, beginning with the *Cantos*, which incorporate creative interpretation of the (textual) past into the ongoing act of writing and reading that only ends with the death of the poet. Browning's idea of the reader's "co-operating fancy" is, if not the first, an early step in the evolution of this mode of discourse. We may distinguish Browning from the reader-orientation of the earlier Romantics also. When Charles Lamb, for instance, writes to Coleridge to praise a line in "Religious Musings," he speaks of "those noble Hints at which the Reader's imagination is apt to Kindle into grand conceptions."[43] Browning's hints are of a different kind. Lamb speaks of the re-imaging in the reader; the spark furnishes an incentive to picture in the mind a grand conception, and the mechanism is associative. Browning's poem is structured around gaps which, on the reader's side, may produce "actors of your own" to try against *Sordello*; it is oriented towards communication that will create the "after-gust."

Browning's "communication different" may be seen then as a bold attempt to exploit the inevitable asymmetries between text and reader, and, by recognizing the limitations of knowledge (especially linguistically structured knowledge) make the reading of the poem into an inter-action rather than a straightforward relationship of power between teller and told. But Browning was over-bold, as he feared, and it is little wonder that readers made sarcastic comments, got headaches, and even feared for their sanity. The fissures of communication, however, haunt many writers during Browning's decade of composition. Arthur Hallam's prose, to cite one example, quickens when he comes to the topic in his otherwise dry "Essay of Cicero":

> How little, in fact, does one creature know of another, even if he lives with him, sees him constantly, and, in popular language, knows all about him! Of that immense chain of mental successions, which extend from the cradle to the death-bed, how few links, comparatively speaking, are visible to any other person! Yet from these fragments of being (if the expression may be pardoned) you shall hear one decide as confidently about the unseen and unimagined whole, as a geologist from his chip of stone will explain the structure of the mass to which it belonged, and even the changes of fortune which it has received at the hands of time.[44]

Browning gives us "fragments of being" (unpardonable for his time), and forces the reader's hand to the task of reconstruction, like the geologist with his chip, or the archeologist with his artifacts. It is the road by which Browning himself approaches the problem of Sordello's "historical" existence in the chronicles, legends, and fictions available to him as a poet-creator. Browning, I think, in his attempt to demonstrate the frailty of the fragmentary links between beings offers us the act of reading itself, for those who will. His poem is the foremost extension of Romantic poetics of difficulty, including the necessity of the "fit audi-ence" paradigm and rigorous exercise of the reader's faculties. It aims to make us ask ourselves, as the narrator asks Sordello, if we are the same reader at the beginning as at the end. Browning's completion of *Sordello*, however, does not end his experimentation; in the epilogue I hope to sketch a few of the ways in which Sordello's story extends into Browning's next work.

"Pippa Passes"

"What other meaning do these verses bear?"

Browning's *Bells and Pomegranates* are often looked upon as a consequence of the failure of *Sordello*, but this is an erroneous connection to make with regards to *Pippa Passes*, unless one refers only to the inexpensive mode of publication. The most important thing to remember about *Pippa Passes* is that Browning began it while still engaged with the longer poem; "A king lived long ago," Pippa's lyric in Part III, was published in *The Monthly Repository* in November of 1835, and most of the poem was probably composed between that date and the end of 1840. In their pioneering biography of Browning, Griffin and Minchen note many of the parallels, and state that "*Pippa*, indeed, seems to have been conceived as a direct contrast to *Sordello*."[1] But the impetus is not merely contrastive. The poem serves, I believe, as another ironic exemplum, or parallel narrative (though one complicated by its unique form as a series of parallel narratives), to the main movement of *Sordello*, and Browning is careful to make this clear through brief hinges, allusions, and suggestive contrasts.

Clyde de L. Ryals is one of the few recent critics to note the connection to *Sordello* in any detail, observing that when Browning breaks the poem in Book III to muse on the palace step in Venice, the girls "Perhaps from our delicious Asolo" (III, 683) are the immediate instigation of his poetic reorientation. Ryals concludes that, "Fresh from the Italian background of *Sordello*, Browning decided to set his new poem again in Northeastern Italy, not however during the early Renaissance but during the contemporary period, the very time of the personal digression in *Sordello*, book three."[2] But this connection is left undeveloped, and *Pippa* is treated in a chapter with *King Victor and King Charles*. The consistent tendency among those who have surveyed Browning's early career has been, in fact, to place *Pippa* among Browning's stage plays, even when it is recognized that it is a closet drama at best. It makes more sense, I think, to see it as the pendant to *Sordello* much as *Paracelsus* is its preface. In the opening lines of *Sordello* the speaker contradicts his own practice in that poem by valuing a better expedient, one in which the writer would produce the story "By making speak, myself kept out of view, / The very man as he was wont to do, / And leaving you to say the rest for him" (I, 15-17). Both *Paracelsus* and *Pippa* are cast as dramas of this kind, and the protagonists are ironic inversions of each other, with Paracelsus claiming immense powers and having none, and Pippa claiming nothing but inadvertently effecting much. One of the difficulties critics have had with *Pippa* is that, after the perplexities of *Sordello*, there doesn't seem to be much "rest" to say about a lucent, rigidly structured play with a simple moral: all service ranks the same with God.

Early readers, such as Mrs. Cook and Mrs. Orr, accept the poem as a sincere rendition of Browning's religious faith; it is Pippa-in-bronze, after all, who guards the portals of the Armstrong Browning Library, with the poet's most famous lines engraved beneath. An excerpt from Mrs. Orr's plot summary is instructive; after Pippa sings in Part I, "Something in her song strikes [Sebald's] conscience like a thunderbolt, and its reviving force awakens Ottima's also. Both are spiritually saved."[3] Most recent critics have reacted against such a view, and have focussed on the ironies in the poem, though they sometimes seem to perceive these ironies in relation to the history of Browning scholarship rather than the work's immediate context.[4] But in 1849 Browning added a line immediately prior to the New Year's hymn, and we would do well to ask the same question of the entire work: "What other meaning do these verses bear?" (Intro., 189).

Another meaning may be found, I think, by taking Ryals' hint and placing *Pippa Passes* within the context of *Sordello*, Book III. The narrator breaks in the middle of Book III to say, "They sleep, and I awake / O'er the lagune. Sordello said once, note" (614-15). A "note" on poetics follows, in which the speaker contrasts Eglamor's poetics of completeness (or what he imagines completeness to be) with the "true works" of Sordello's own "dream performances." (The speaker, we should mention, has just awakened from a dream performance, presumably the rest of his unfinished poem.) Once again, poetry is bifurcated into two varying, mutually exclusive paths, though this be an illusion and both paths meet again at the starting point. A metaphor follows of the poem as a river, its narrative line slinking like a stream of print in which "The margin's silent" (657). This may harken back to the opening desire for poetry depersonalized, "myself kept out of view," though ironically *Sordello* has for the moment become all marginalia. The reader is next addressed directly, in lines that obliquely question the contemporary act of reading as exemplified in the aesthetics of ease, and then we are presented with the most specific scene in the metatext yet, a passage replete with deictic markers and present tense questionings. It is worth quoting in full:

> Wherefore? Ah yes, we frolic it to-day:
> To-morrow, and the pageant's moved away
> Down to the poorest tent-pole: we and you
> Part company: no other may pursue
> Eastward your voyage, be informed what fate
> Intends, if triumph or decline await
> The tempter of the everlasting steppe.
>   I sung this on an empty palace-step
> At Venice: why should I break off, nor sit
> Longer upon my step, exhaust the fit
> England gave birth to? Who's adorable
> Enough reclaim a —— no Sordello's Will
> Alack! — be queen to me? That Bassanese
> Busied among her smoking fruit-boats? These
> Perhaps from our delicious Asolo
> Who twinkle, pigeons o'er the portico
> Not prettier, bind late lilies into sheaves
> To deck the bridge-side chapel, dropping leaves
> Soiled by their own loose gold-meal? Ah, beneath
> The cool arch stoops she, brownest-cheek! Her wreath
> Endures a month — a half month — if I make
> A queen of her, continue for her sake
> Sordello's story? Nay, that Paduan girl
> Splashes with barer legs where a live whirl
> In the dead black Giudecca proves sea-weed
> Drifting has sucked down three, four, all indeed
> Save one pale-red striped, pale-blue turbaned post
> For gondolas.   (III, 669-96)

Browning has broken off his sample "pageant poem" convinced that these poems provide no after-gust, that no one should care about an exotic hero, the "tempter of the everlasting steppe." (One is tempted to see here the remains of a *Sordello* that traced the epic actions of the poet as warrior-chief, whose legendary exploits are mentioned in Book VI, 822-29.) Writing — recollecting — the moment that he "sung this on an empty palace step," the speaker associates the steppe of action with the "step" of an empty (queenless) palace, and finally with the metaphor of the step, or the action that advances the individual and the race upwards and forwards — as in "the step too mean for him to take" that Sordello misses. It is a Venice, as Lawrence Poston notes, in which "not only are Venetian power and influence gone, but also the Byronic idea of Venice, the later romanticization of that power and influence."[5] Returning to the metaphoric terms of Book I, Browning sees a locale almost all sea-wrack, in which sea-weed is sucking down aristocratic gondola posts — rather than eroding cliffs. The speaker/Browning looks now for his own equivalent of Palma (though the irony of Palma's ghibelline — cliff or "post" — politics is not lost), and casts his youthful eye over the girls gathered about the lagune. The most mangled line is the most interesting: "Who's adorable / Enough reclaim a —— no Sordello's Will / Alack! — be queen to me?" (679-81). This is poetry that is not meant to be readily understood, and Browning allowed it to stand without revision. Exactly what the interjection signifies is not known; the "queen to me" however may be referred to *Pippa Passes*, in which a poor girl from Asolo assumes regal status.

Samuel Chell notes that *Pippa* "may be seen as a reaction against the intellectual obscurities and arcane language of" *Sordello*.[6] This may be true as regards style, especially syntax; but I think that its own intellectual complexities are unfurled when it is placed in conjunction with the earlier poem, and Pippa's "Introduction" in the 1841 text continues with *Sordello* style. In a moment of poetic crisis in which the speaker flounders to re-orient the poem for the service of the people, the parallel and contemporary structure of Pippa's "service" is an ironic counterpoint to the entire effort of writing *Sordello*. The passage in Book III continues, "You sad disheveled ghost / That pluck at me and point," and this ghost gains shape as both an individual Italian girl and a personification of suffering humanity (Browning's letter to Haworth — May, 1840; *New Letters*, pp. 18-19 — one might add, hedges perhaps out of delicacy for refined feeling the extent to which the girl is present in the flesh). The girl is perceived as a beggar-girl like Pippa, who describes in her "Introduction" how such girls, although "flower-like," "have to trip along the streets like me / All but naked to the knee!" (152-53). This "passing" down the street echoes *Sordello*, Book III, in which Browning addresses the Italian girl:

> Ah, had I, judge,
> Or no, your secret? Rough apparel — grudge
> All ornaments save tag or tassel worn
> To hint we are not thoroughly forlorn —

> Slouch bonnet, unloop mantle, careless go
> Alone (that's saddest but it must be so)
> Through Venice, sing now and now glance aside,
> Aught desultory or undignified,
> And, ravishingest lady, will you pass
> Or not each formidable group, the mass
> Before the Basilike (that feast gone by,
> God's day, the great June Corpus Domini)
> And wistfully foregoing proper men,
> Come timid up to me for alms?   (III, 755-68)

The speaker watches this girl pass by groups and sing, though without an inkling of the presence of an effect upon the audience. That the poet at this moment has found his "queen" is evident, and the "people" as represented in the "sad disheveled ghost" are both powerful in their own right, and powerful as they legitimize the speaker's song.

One of Browning's revisions to Book III of 1863 demonstrates the subtle ways in which he wished to connect the two poems at the Venetian digression; after the girl falls asleep (III, 784ff.) we are privy to an interior colloquy of poets and poetry, a kind of inner-digested precursors' song. Poets are classed into three groups, and the last, "the best / Impart the gift of seeing to the rest"; we are given "a deed in proof" of this class, a portion of a poem by a poet, jailed in Venice, who re-imagines his mistress stooping to go beneath some hazel branches. The last lines in 1840 read:

> Thus, prisoned in the Piombi, I repeat
> Events one rove occasioned, o'er and o'er,
> Putting 'twixt me and madness evermore
> Thy sweet shape, Elys! therefore stoop —   (III, 876-79)

Elys, of course, is the name given to the ideal, imaginary queen of the poem by both Eglamor and Sordello. The name thus refers to the story of *Sordello*, and the "best" is connected to troubadour poetics, and seemingly placed in the distant past. Mason finds in this passage an allusion by Browning to Landor's treatment of the imprisonment of Tasso, implying a recognition of Landor's "technique of vivid sympathetic entry into human predicaments," as well as Tasso's poetics.[7] But in 1863 Browning changed the last line to read, "Thy sweet shape, Zanze! Therefore Stoop!" Here we see a much more apparent allusion, for Zanze is the name of the most outspoken and pert of the Italian girls who attempt, at the instigation of Bluphocks, to lead Pippa down the road to ruin. Pippa's final monologue, alone in her darkened chamber, deals largely with her remembrance of the conversation with Zanze; for her, since the other effects of her song are unknown, this has been the most significant encounter of the day, and it leads her to a statement of the doctrine of evolution of the spirit that has been such a large part of *Sordello*. Picking up a flower to call a "heart's-ease" (IV,ii, 59) for her lily, Pippa recognizes the improvements of flower-breeders; her fancy takes her from there:

> Suppose there's a king of the flowers
> And a girl-show held in his bowers —
> "Look ye, buds, this growth of ours,"
> Says he, "Zanze from the Brenta,
> I have made her gorge polenta
> Till both cheeks are near as bouncing
> As her... name there's no pronouncing!
> See this heightened colour too —
> For she swilled Breganze wine
> Till her nose turned deep Carmine —
> 'Twas but white when wild she grew!
> And only by this Zanze's eyes
> Of which we could not change the size,
> The magnitude of what's achieved
> Elsewhere may be perceived!"   (IV, ii, 67-81)

Pippa's prognosis of devolution in the "girl-show" is ironically juxtaposed with the improvements in flower breeding; though Pippa resents the other girl and envies her attire, a consideration of the plight of Zanze ends Pippa's day, and, as Browning has shown in his rededication of the poem to the girl in *Sordello* III, a concern for the Zanzes of the world is the proper end of poetry as well. The "best" poet is one who can make others see her plight, even if it lands him in the Piombi where he must imagine Zanze stoop over and over again. Changing "Elys" to "Zanze" is a significant additional connection of *Sordello* to *Pippa Passes*, one that reinforces many of the connections already made, and one that through the parallels between *Pippa* and the girls by the canal suggests that the "Queen" of Book III borders on becoming a prostitute.

In a recent essay, "Notes for a History of Victorian Poetic Genres," Avrom Fleishman finds that the Victorians make very few references to "contemporary politics, world-historical events, social movements, etc." but that Italian nationalist politics is an exception.[8] The sublimation of the ravishing Italian girl here into the ghost of the suffering masses (to stimulate, according to the letter to Haworth, "Republicanism") is one of the moments in which both politics and sexuality become turned in Victorian poetry into the energies of the poem. The masses, in an era of chartist rallies, hardly need personifying or placement in the past, and the narrator's first interest in the girls — perhaps like too many other Englishmen on tour — is their difference from the English middle-class norms. A similar tension, almost a variation and explanation of this part of *Sordello*, may be found in "The Englishman in Italy," from *Dramatic Romances and Lyrics* (1845), in which the speaker begins with the desire to make the Italian girl Fortù laugh, and ends with a rare allusion to contemporary politics (the Corn Law debate). Browning's digression in *Sordello* unveils a new dimension to the speaker's act, as it marks the metamorphosis of the individual erotic motive — as in some Romantic poems by Byron, Shelley, and Keats, or Browning's *Pauline* — into the assumption of responsibility for love gone awry; the theme becomes a collective, Carlylean concern for suffering mankind. In his lengthy summary of Carlyle's philosophy in 1839, Sterling notes how "The dusky millions of human shapes that flit around us, and in history stream away, fill him with an almost passionate sorrow. Their hunger and nakedness, their mistakes, terrors, pangs, and ignorances, press upon his soul like personal calamities."[9] Browning's "sad disheveled ghost" is one of these, but first she is an object of desire, and next a "queen"; this latter role is one appropriated by Pippa, that highly unrealistic factory girl.

We may now turn to *Pippa Passes* to see the conjunction of a naive poetry that surpasses in power the constructions of both types of self-conscious poets analyzed at such great lengths in Book II of *Sordello*. As we have seen, in the fertile climate for poetic theory of the 1830s, ideas about the ultimate power of the poet abounded; one of the most extreme descends from Schiller's discussion of the naive versus sentimental orders of genius. Carlyle draws heavily on Schiller to praise Goethe, but with the implication that his natural genius is no longer possible in a more self-conscious age. Browning's poets in *Sordello* are all self-conscious, and only Salinguerra, through his Renaissance *sprezzatura*, comes close to being a naive genius in Schiller's sense. But at the moment of the speaker's championing of his urchin queen we have the implied expression of this mode in the parallel story of *Pippa Passes*. Schiller writes,

> By this naive grace genius expresses its most sublime and profound thought; the utterances of a god in the mouth of a child. . . . genius delineates its own thoughts at a single felicitous stroke of the brush with an equally determined,

firm, and absolutely free outline.... As freely and naturally as genius expresses itself in its works of the spirit, its innocence of heart is expressed in its social intercourse.[10]

Pippa arises on her New Year's Day equipped with the potential of this form of genius, determined to escape the silence of the girl in Book III, as well as Fortù in "An Englishman in Italy." Each discussion, each ironic twist in the allowance of the poet's power to affect the audience in *Sordello* is shadowed by Pippa, who in this sense passes through the earlier poem, too. Her first song must be seen as an interlude that connects her story with the ending of *Sordello*, as well as an itinerary for her day's royal progress.

Pippa is prefigured most emphatically in *Sordello* at the very end of the poem. Late in Book VI, the speaker recounts details of the scene of the poem as viewed in contemporary times; it is a doubling of vision, and a doubling of discourse in which the reader enacts the choice of what is pertinent or valuable to the poem. "I take / God's part," he says, to testify to the remains of the landscape; but in a poem of portentous parables and choices, what follows seems rankly anticlimactic:

> there, at deep of day
> A week since, heard I the old Canon say
> He saw with his own eyes a barrow burst
> And Alberic's huge skeleton unhearsed
> Five years ago, no more: he added, June's
> A month for carding off our first cocoons
> The silkworms fabricate — a double news,
> Nor he nor I could tell the worthier. Choose!   (VI, 789-96)

The past, irrelevant, anecdotal, is placed against the rhythm of the year; we are in the Italy of silk-winders and the "people." The speaker then reiterates the idea that the world would have been drastically changed if Sordello had seized his "step" — he would have compassed Apollo, and men would eat Hesperian fruit. But the beginnings of Sordello's step in his imaginative re-creation of Eglamor's "Elys" song are available to the present day, which is one reading of the action that follows, as the speaker directs us "this way — " (VI, 852) to a new locale, the little town of Asolo, where he chances to overhear a boy singing a portion of the "Elys" song, the origin of which we assume the boy is ignorant. Many commentators have noticed the obvious connection to *Pippa Passes*, but again only circumstantially.[11] The incident is usually interpreted as a final ironic comment by the speaker on Sordello's aspirations; only a

129

small part of his least original work is remembered and sung as a folk song. But the context allows a much stronger interpretation.

> Lo, on a heathy brown and nameless hill
> By sparkling Asolo, in mist and chill,
> Morning just up, higher and higher runs
> A child barefoot and rosy — See! the sun's
> On the square castle's inner-court's green wall
> — Like the chine of some fossil animal
> Half turned to earth and flowers; and thro' the haze
> (Save where some slender patches of grey maize
> Are to be overleaped) that boy has crost
> The whole hill-side of dew and powder-frost
> Matting the balm and mountain camomile:
> Up and up goes he, singing all the while
> Some unintelligible words to beat
> The lark, God's poet, swooning at his feet
> So worsted is he at the few fine locks
> Stained like pale honey oozed from topmost rocks
> Sunblanched the livelong summer. — All that's left
> Of the Goito lay! And thus bereft,
> Sleep and forget, Sordello...   (VI, 850-71)

The speaker turns then from ridiculing Sordello's failure to become "Apollo," to overhearing a song — a naive performance that may be glossed by the passage from Schiller, "the utterance of a god in the mouth of a child." Does Sordello live for some one better thing? The failure to seize the moment for action has not meant inaction, as long as any portion of his poetry (or his joy) exists; the effect of the "Goito lay" at such a distance makes the the boy not Apollo, but Orpheus, making the larks to swoon. In this passage we see Sordello's "art" becoming nature, the fossils (the skeletons of the past, of Alberic) metamorphosing into flowers, and the "unintelligible" words rippling into the aftergust as they are overheard.

The boy is, however, Pippa's fellow townsman from Asolo, and the "square castle's inner-court" is the turret of "La Roca" where Luigi will meet his mother to decide upon regicide. The boy sings at the spot where Pippa will pass by, where she will recite verses as traditional as the snatch of Sordello's Goito lay; it is a seamless turn from here to another (or the same?) flower-filled morning in Asolo when Pippa arises to hymn her day:

Day!
Faster and more fast
O'er night's brim day boils at last;
Boils, pure gold, o'er the cloud-cup's brim
Where spurting and supprest it lay —
For not a froth-flake touched the rim
Of yonder gap in the solid gray
Of eastern cloud an hour away —
But forth one wavelet then another curled,
.Till the whole sunrise, not to be supprest,
Rose-reddened, and its seething breast
Flickered in bounds, grew gold, then overflowed the world.

(Intro. 1-12)

Pippa's singing is reminiscent of the confident verse movement of the
opening of Shelley's *The Triumph of Life* in its recreation of the power of
the sunrise. As personified in the dawn, Day completely fills the world,
and the divine power of this plenum is matched by Pippa, whose
opening contrasts sharply with the self-conscious speaker's inability to
begin in *Sordello*. Like the boy of Asolo's recital of the Elys song, this is
pure poetry in which the singer is unaware of any audience. In 1833 the
young John Stuart Mill made a distinction between poetry and eloquence in an essay in *The Monthly Repository*, which, as Clyde Ryals has
noted, has a relevance to *Pippa Passes*; Mill writes,

> Poetry and eloquence are both alike the expression or utterance of feeling.
> But if we may excuse the antithesis, we should say that eloquence is *heard*,
> poetry is *over*heard. Eloquence supposes an audience; the peculiarity of
> poetry appears to lie in the poet's utter unconsciousness of a listener. Poetry is
> feeling expressing itself to itself, in moments of solitude, and embodying itself
> in symbols which are the nearest possible representations of the feeling in the
> exact shape in which it exists in the poet's mind. Eloquence is feeling pouring
> itself out to other minds, courting their sympathy, or endeavoring to
> influence their belief or move them to passion or action.[12]

Pippa's daybreak song closely fulfills this ideal, and links her and the boy
of Asolo to the youthful Sordello of Goito in the "sunrise of blossoming
and May," before he is aware "others desired a portion in his joy" (I, 297
& 686).

Because she consciously plans her day, however, Pippa's song, like
Sordello's boyhood fantasies, quickly "rehearses the future" (*Sordello* I,
846). She knows the stories of Asolo's four happiest ones, plans to become
them, and deliberately sings at the moment she passes by, so we must

131

assume that her subsequent songs partake of the nature of eloquence, "courting their sympathy... endeavoring to influence their belief or move them to passion or action." Her own ideal, however, is that of absolute identification:

> Laugh thro' my pane then, solicit the bee,
> Gibe him, be sure, and in midst of thy glee
> Worship me!
>
> Worship whom else? For am I not this Day
> Whate'er I please? Who shall I seem to-day?
> Morn, Noon, Eve, Night — how must I spend my Day?
>
> Up the hill-side, thro' the morning,
> Love me as I love!
> I am Ottima, take warning,   (Intro., 101-16)

The identification with the object here reminds us of the poetics described in *Sordello*, Book I, in which we find described poets who function through "A need to blend with each external charm, / Bury themselves, the whole heart wide and warm, / In something not themselves; they would belong / To what they worship" (I, 507-10). This tendency is illustrated through a cosmological "legend" (I, 515ff.) about the entrance of light into the universe; the terms of Pippa's seizure of the Other, combined with the necessity of worship (which also threads through *Sordello*, Book III), place her tale alongside this legend, as Pippa arises with first light.

The two poems exchange such parallelisms and commentary constantly, often through imagery — lark, bee, sunrise, sunset — or more obliquely through the strange consonance of Naddo and Bluphocks, Pippa and Sordello, Zanze and Elys. At the moment that Sordello dies, "By this, the hermit-bee has stopped / His day's toil at Goito" (VI, 621-22); Pippa orders his flowery dominions to "solicit" this insect, and the erratic yet fruitful flights of meaning between these poems are adequately emblemed by the bee's cross-pollination in its quest to make honey. Browning's poetics of difficulty extend into *Pippa Passes*, and a complete reading of this drama would extend Pippa's creed — "there is no last nor first" — to the acts of reading engendered by Browning's early poetry.

NOTES

NOTES TO THE INTRODUCTION

1 *New Letters of Thomas Carlyle*, ed. Alexander Carlyle (London: John Lane, 1904), 1, p. 233.

2 *The Collected Letters of Thomas and Jane Welsh Carlyle*, ed. C. R. Sanders, Kenneth T. Fielding, et al. (Durham, NC: Duke University Press, 1970 — in progress), 9, p. 15 (Letter to J. S. Mill, 22 July, 1836).

3 Pauline Fletcher, *Gardens and Grim Ravines: The Language of Landscape in Victorian Poetry* (Princeton: Princeton University Press, 1983), p. xi. Browning called the poem a "monster" himself in a letter to William Dow in 1837; see *Correspondence*, 3, p. 280.

4 Thomas J. Collins, *Robert Browning's Moral-Aesthetic Theory, 1833-1855* (Lincoln: University of Nebraska Press, 1967), pp. 45-46.

5 Lionel Stevenson, "The Key Poem of the Victorian Age," in *Essays in American and English Literature Presented to Bruce Robert McElderry, Jr.* (Athens: Ohio University Press, 1967), p. 266.

6 Morse Peckham, *Romanticism and Behavior: Collected Essays II* (Columbia: University of South Carolina Press, 1976); from an essay on *The Ring in the Book* published in *Victorian Poetry* in 1968.

NOTES TO CHAPTER ONE
READING AND THE AESTHETICS OF DIFFICULTY

1 J. A. Wittreich, "Opening the Seals: Blake's Epics and the Miltonic Tradition," in *Blake's Sublime Allegory* (Madison: University of Wisconsin Press, 1973), p. 40. Sir Walter Scott, *The Life of John Dryden*, ed. Bernard Kreissman (1808; Lincoln: University of Nebraska Press, 1963), p. 48.

2 *The Romantic Poems of Sir Walter Scott* (London: Thomas Nelson, 1910), 2, pp. 587-88.

3 William Hazlitt, *Lectures on the English Poets and The Spirit of the Age* (New York: E. P. Dutton, 1910), p. 336.

4 *British Review*, May, 1813; rpt. in John O. Hayden, ed., *Scott: The Critical Heritage* (New York: Barnes & Noble, 1970), pp. 63-64.

5 Thomas Love Peacock, *Letters to Edward Hookham and Percy B. Shelley*, ed. Richard Garnett (Boston: The Bibliophile Society, 1910), p. 90.

6 [John Gibson Lockhart], "Philip van Artevelde," *Quarterly Review*, 51 (1834), 378-80.

7 Marilyn Butler, *Romantics, Rebels and Reactionaries: English Literature and Its Background: 1760-1830* (New York: Oxford University Press, 1982), p. 91.

8 John Dryden, *Essays*, ed. W. P. Ker (London: Oxford University Press, 1926), 2, p. 225.

9 "Prospectus to *The Reflector*," in *Prefaces by Leigh Hunt*, ed. R. Brimley Johnson (1927; Port Washington, NY: Kennikat Press, 1967), pp. 45-46.

10 I quote from the prospectus as printed with various ms. versions in the appendix to M. H. Abrams, *Natural Supernaturalism* (New York: Norton, 1971), p. 466.

11 Scott, *Life of Dryden*, p. 1.

12 *Literary Criticism of William Wordsworth*, ed. Paul M. Zall (Lincoln: University of Nebraska Press, 1966), p. 182. Future references in text.

13 Samuel Taylor Coleridge, *Biographia Literaria*, ed. George Watson (London: Dent, 1975), p. 267.

14 Professor Wilson, *Noctes Ambrosianae* (Philadelphia: 1843), 1, pp. 364-65.

15 *The Letters of Percy Bysshe Shelley*, ed. Frederick Jones (Oxford: Clarendon Press, 1964), 2, p. 174.

16 *Journal of Edward Ellerker Williams* (London: Elkin Matthews, 1902), p. 24.

17 *Letters of Percy Bysshe Shelley*, 2, p. 263.

18 Shelley, *Poetical Works*, ed. Hutchinson and Matthews (New York: Oxford University Press, 1970), p. 411.

19 Hazlitt, "Sismondi and the Trecentisti" (1815), in Beatrice Corrigan, ed., *Italian Poets and English Critics, 1755-1859* (Chicago: University of Chicago Press, 1969), p. 58.

20 Leigh Hunt, *Lord Byron and Some of His Contemporaries* (1828); excerpted in Theodore Redpath, *The Young Romantics and Critical Opinion, 1807-1824* (London: Harrap, 1973), pp. 409-10.

21 Shelley, *Poetical Works*, p. xxiii.

22 [William Henry Smith], "The Poets of Our Age, Considered as to their Philosophic Tendencies," *Westminster Review*, 25 (1836), 69.

23 *The Collected Letters of Thomas and Jane Welsh Carlyle*, 9, pp. 125 & 219; 8, pp. 12 & 209.

24 *The Writings of Arthur Hallam*, ed. T. H. Vail Motter (New York: Modern Language Association, 1943), pp. 184 & 198.

25 See John Maynard, *Browning's Youth* (Cambridge: Harvard University Press, 1977), especially "Shelley Discovered: 'A Spell to Me Alone,'" pp. 193-200; also, for a more general account of the burst of enthusiasm for Shelley among the new generation, Sylva Norman, *Flight of the Skylark: The Development of Shelley's Reputation* (London: Max Reinhardt, 1954), especially "A Rally of Youth," pp. 83-106.

26 Richard Hengist Horne, ed., *A New Spirit of the Age* (London: Oxford University Press, 1907), pp. 243-45.

27 [J. Heraud?], "A Cambrian Colloquy on the Decline and Fall of Poetry," *Fraser's Magazine*, 10 (1834), 650.

28 *The Collected Writings of Thomas de Quincey*, ed. David Masson (London: 1896-1898), 10, p. 395.

29 Georges Poulet, "The Phenomenology of Reading," *New Literary History* 1, (1969), 57.

30 See Richard Macksey, "The Consciousness of the Critic: Georges Poulet and the Reader's Share," in *Velocities of Change: Critical Essays from MLN*, ed. Richard Macksey (Baltimore: The Johns Hopkins University Press, 1974), pp. 319-20.

31 *Prefaces by Leigh Hunt*, p. 43.

32 Quoted in *The Young Romantics*, ed. Redpath, pp. 31-32.

33 *New Letters of Robert Southey*, ed. Kenneth Curray (New York: Columbia University Press, 1965), 2, p. 180.

34 Coleridge, *Poetical Works*, ed. E. H. Coleridge (1912; London: Oxford University Press, 1973), p. 599.

35 Fielding, *Joseph Andrews*, ed. Martin Battestin (Boston: Houghton Mifflin, 1961), p. 190.

36 Sterne, *Tristram Shandy*, ed. Ian Watt (Boston: Houghton Mifflin, 1965), p. 356.

37 *The Letters of William and Dorothy Wordsworth*, ed. Ernest de Selincourt, 2d ed., rev. by Chester Shaver (Oxford: Clarendon Press, 1967), 1, p. 56.

38 *New Letters of Robert Southey*, 1, p. 365.

39 *Essays on the Nature and Principles of Taste*, ed. Abraham Mills (New York: 1852), p. 51.

40 Wordsworth *Poetical Works*, ed. Ernest de Selincourt, 2d ed., rev. by Chester Shaver (Oxford: Clarendon Press, 1967), p. 379.

41 Coleridge, *Biographia Literaria*, p. 173.

42 *Henry Crabb Robinson on Books and Their Writers*, ed. Edith Morley (London: J. M. Dent, 1938), 1, pp. 27 & 29.

43 Samuel Rogers, *Poems* (London: 1834), p. 217.

44 S. T. Coleridge, *Inquiring Spirit*, ed. Kathleen Coburn (New York: Minerva Press, 1968), p. 104.

45 *The Writings of Arthur Hallam*, p. 188.

46 Coleridge, *Inquiring Spirit*, p. 104; from a letter to the *Courier*, 21 September, 1811.

47 John Stuart Mill, *Literary Essays*, ed. Edward Alexander (Indianapolis: Bobbs-Merrill, 1967), p. 132.

48 Lord Byron, *Selected Poems and Letters*, ed. William Marshall (Boston: Houghton Mifflin, 1968), p. 368.

49 *The Complete Poetry and Prose of William Blake*, ed. David V. Erdman, newly rev. ed. (Berkeley: University of California Press, 1982), p. 524.

50 Quoted in Tzvetan Todorov, *Theories of the Symbol*, trans. C. Porter (Ithaca: Cornell University Press, 1982), p. 187.

51 "Specimans of German Genius," ed. and trans. Sarah Austin, *New Monthly Magazine*, 29 (130), 183-85.

52 Wolfgang Iser, *The Act of Reading: A Theory of Aesthetic Response* (Baltimore: The Johns Hopkins University Press, 1978), p. 27. Future references cited in the text.

53 Iser, "Interview," conducted by R. E. Kuenzli, *Diacritics*, 10 (1982), 65.

54 Fish, "Why No One's Afraid of Wolfgang Iser," *Diacritics*, 11 (1981), 4.

55 Barnouw, "Rev. of *The Act of Reading* and *The Implied Reader*, by Wolfgang Iser," *MLN*, 94 (1979), 1211. One of Fish's points, it should be mentioned, is that no one fears the critical theory of Wolfgang Iser because he offers something for everyone. Since Fish and Barnouw find mutually exclusive faults in Iser's theory, this may be true. For a study of the relationship of Iser to Ingarden see Horst Ruthrof, *The Reader's Construction of Narrative* (London: Routledge & Kegan Paul, 1981).

56 John Wilson, *Noctes Ambrosianae* 2, p. 27.

57 "The Reading Process: A Phenomenological Approach," *New Literary History*, 3 (1972), 295. Future references cited in the text as "Reading Process."

58 Coleridge, *Poetical Works*, p. 48.

59 Fish argues, of course, that the stars themselves are not fixed; their position, too, is subject to interpretation (p. 7).

60 In *Robert Browning: A Collection of Critical Essays*, ed. Harold Bloom and Adrienne Munich (Englewood Cliffs, NJ: Prentice Hall, 1979), p. 106.

61 Ian Jack, "Browning on *Sordello* and *Men and Women*: Unpublished Letters to James T. Fields," *Huntington Library Quarterly*, 45 (1982), 196.

NOTES TO CHAPTER TWO
AUDIENCES IN AND AUDIENCES OUT OF *SORDELLO*

1 William Henry Smith, "Philip van Artevelde," *Westminster Review*, 25 (1836), 170. By "symbolic writing" Smith refers to hieroglyphs. In an important new essay, "Poetry as Pure Act: A Coleridgean Ideal in Early Victorian England," Lawrence Poston shows the relation of Smith's statement to a Coleridgean view of a poetics in which "as nearly as possible the word stands directly for the thing, the image is incarnate in the word, the word coterminous with the image." *Modern Philology*, 84 (1986), 181-82.

2 These quotations are from reviews in *The Dublin Review* and *The Metropolitan Magazine*; see Litzinger and Smalley, eds., *Browning: The Critical Heritage* (London: Routledge & Kegan Paul, 1970), pp. 63, 66.

3 John Edmund Reade, *Cain the Wanderer: A Vision of Heaven: Darkness; and other Poems* (London: 1829), p. 7.

⁴ Jauss, *Toward an Aesthetic of Reception*, trans. by Timothy Bahti, intro. by Paul de Man (Minneapolis: University of Minnesota Press, 1982), p. 19.

⁵ See Alan J. Chaffee, "Dialogue and Dialectic in Browning's *Sordello*," *TSLL*, 23 (1981), 52-77; Chaffee emphasizes the similarity between the dialogic in Browning and the exchanges of psychiatry. Loy D. Martin in *Browning's Dramatic Monologues and the Post-Romantic Subject* (Baltimore: The Johns Hopkins University Press, 1985), examines the dialogic modes of Browning's monologues through a marxist analysis of the transition from Romantic to Victorian subjectivity.

⁶ Lee Erickson, *Robert Browning: His Poetry and His Audiences* (Ithaca, NY: Cornell University Press, 1984), p. 63.

⁷ Karl Kroeber, *Romantic Narrative Art* (Madison: University of Wisconsin Press, 1960), p. 7.

⁸ John Stuart Mill, "The Two Kinds of Poetry" (1833); in *Literary Essays*, p. 72.

⁹ Carlyle's admonition in *Sartor* is well known; see also Patrick Creevy, "The Victorian Goethe Critics: Notions of Greatness and Development," *Victorians Institute Journal*, 13 (1985), 30-57.

¹⁰ This problem is addressed, though not resolved, by Robert R. Columbus and Claudette Kemper in "Sordello and the Speaker: A Problem of Identity," *Victorian Poetry*, 2 (1964), 251-67.

¹¹ William Irvine and Park Honan, *The Book, the Ring, and the Poet* (New York: McGraw Hill, 1974), p. 92.

¹² See Mark D. Hawthorne, "Browning, *Sordello* and *Don Quixote*," *MLN*, 92 (1977), 1033-37, for an analysis of this allusion.

¹³ See Stempel, "Browning's *Sordello* and the Art of the Makers-see," *PMLA*, 80 (1965), 554-61, for a suggestion that the speaker assumes the posture of a showman at a diorama; I argue against this view in "The Diorama 'Showman' in *Sordello*," *Studies in Browning and His Circle*, 14 (1986).

¹⁴ The "narratee" (*narrataire*) is Gerald Prince's proposed term for this phenomenon; see "Introduction to the study of the Narratee," in Jane Tompkins, ed., *Reader-Response Criticism*, pp. 7-25. See also Seymour Chatman, *Narrative Structure in Fiction and Film* (Ithaca: Cornell University Press, 1978), 146-95.

¹⁵ Peter Rabinowitz, "Truth in Fiction: A Reexamination of Audiences," *Critical Inquiry*, 4 (1977), 127.

¹⁶ Hunt, *Captain Sword and Captain Pen* (London, 1835; published in facsimile, Iowa City: Friends of the University of Iowa Libraries, 1984), p. 9.

¹⁷ Prince, "Introduction to the Study of the Narratee," 15-16.

¹⁸ Shelley, *Critical Prose*, ed. Bruce McElderry (Lincoln: University of Nebraska Press, 1967), p. 11. It is tempting to believe that Browning knew of the "Defence" before his poem was completed. The "Defence" was first published in *Essays, Letters from Abroad, Translations and Fragments* (1840), but the volume was in reviewers' hands in December of 1839. Furthermore, Mary Shelley's intimacy with Moxon in 1838-40 coincides with Browning's move-

ments in the same circle. Moxon published *Sordello* as well as Mary Shelley's editions of her husband's works, and there is evidence that Browning assisted Moxon in the preparation of the editions of Shelley's works. Peacock, however, had custody of the manuscript of the "Defence," and it wasn't until July of 1839 that Mary Shelley wrote Mary Ellen Peacock to ask for it for the new edition. See *The Letters of Mary Wollstonecraft Shelley*, ed. Betty T. Bennett (Baltimore: The Johns Hopkins University Press, 1983), 2, pp. 232, 323 & 325.

[19] For commentary on the digression in Book III, see especially Isobel Armstrong, *Language as Living Form in Nineteenth-Century Poetry*, chap. 5, "Browning, the fracture of subject and object: *Sordello*, Book III" (Totowa, NJ: Barnes & Noble, 1982), pp. 141-71; and Linda H. Peterson, "Biblical Typology and the Self Portrait of the Poet in Robert Browning," in *Approaches to Victorian Autobiography*, ed. George P. Landow (Athens: Ohio University Press, 1979), pp. 235-68.

[20] Quoted in William Clyde DeVane, *A Browning Handbook*, 2d ed. (New York: Appleton-Century-Crofts, 1955), p. 79. Christine Froula, for instance, says "the autobiographical digression [was] composed during his 1838 pilgrimage to the Italian scenes where *Sordello* is set" — "Browning's *Sordello* and the Parables of Modernist Poetics," *ELH*, 52 (1985), 970.

[21] George Steiner, *On Difficulty and Other Essays* (Oxford: Oxford University Press, 1978), p. 35.

[22] These lines represent some of the pitfalls of interpretation presented by Browning's attempt to clarify the poem in 1863. Line 615 in the first version concludes "O'er the lagune. Sordello said once, note," and the discussion of Eglamor which follows is clearly in Sordello's voice. In the revision, undoubtedly to establish firmly the setting of the digression, the line reads, "O'er the lagune, being at Venice. Note." But Browning adds no quotation marks as he does elsewhere, and Sordello's lines thus seem to be spoken by the narrator. This section has provoked a wide range of interpretation and paraphrase, including Columbus and Kemper's strange contention that "the Speaker finds himself physically in twelfth century Venice" ("Sordello and the Speaker," 265).

[23] Clyde de L. Ryals, "Browning's Irony," in *The Victorian Experience: The Poets*, ed. Richard Levine (Athens: Ohio University Press, 1982), p. 33.

[24] John Sterling, "Carlyle," in *Essays and Tales*, ed. with a Memoir of his Life by Julius Charles Hare (London: 1848), 2, p. 323.

[25] [Euphrasia Haworth], "Sonnets to the Author of 'Paracelsus,'" *New Monthly Magazine*, 48 (1837), 48.

[26] According to Maynard, these annotations "reveal close reading and serious reflection," and in general "few writers have been lucky enough to have such sympathetic and intelligent friends cheering them on from the sidelines and giving them at least some idea of what an audience might be at its best" (*Browning's Youth*, 110-11).

27 Christine Froula, "Browning's *Sordello* and the Parables of Modernist Poetics," *ELH*, 52 (1986), 971 & 985. The homage to Landor is ambiguous, I think, only if we see Browning denying the validity of any heroic action; the debate between the lyre and crown never denies the validity, say, of Aeschylus's fighting in the battle of Marathon. Her reading of the address to Haworth is also full of problems. Given the closeness of the relationship, I think it is inconceivable that Browning would "gibe" at her in print.

28 Herbert F. Tucker, *Browning's Beginnings: The Art of Disclosure* (Minneapolis: University of Minnesota Press, 1980), p. 101.

29 [John A. Heraud], "On Poetical Genius Considered as a Creative Power," *Fraser's Magazine*, 1 (1830), 60. Browning's own account of his youthful verse-making may be found in a letter to Monclar of 1837 *Correspondence*, 3, pp. 264-66): "I cannot remember the time when I did not make verses and think verse-making the finest thing in the world." The account here in *Sordello* is obliquely revelatory of Browning's own boyhood ambitions.

30 D'Israeli's anatomy of genius first appeared in 1795, then in revisions of 1818, 1822, and 1828. Byron read the 1818 edition and made suggestions which D'Israeli incorporated.

31 Lord Byron, *Selected Poems and Letters*, p. 266. "Lament of Tasso," VI, 149-56.

32 In an interesting essay which posits a dichotomy between the "Apollonian" ideal of Sordello and the "Bacchian" mode of Salinguerra, Alan P. Johnson argues that "Apollo-hood... remains the destiny Sordello should fulfill" — "*Sordello*: Apollo, Bacchus, and the Pattern of Italian History," *Victorian Poetry*, 7 (1969), 326. I would argue that the exact opposite may be true.

33 J. C. L. Simonde di Sismondi, *Historical View of the Literature of the South of Europe*, trans. Thomas Roscoe, 2d ed. (London: 1846), 1, p. 105. A *tenson* is also featured in the climax to L.E.L.'s poem *The Troubadour* (London: 1825).

34 Tucker, *Browning's Beginnings*, p. 17.

35 Baretti's essay is anthologized in *Italian Poets and English Critics*, ed. B, Corrigan, p. 32. For a recent study of Dante's importance to English literature, see Steve Ellis, *Dante and English Poetry: Shelley to T. S. Eliot* (London: Cambridge University Press, 1983), especially chapter three, "Browning, Dante and the two Sordellos," pp. 66-101.

36 In Corrigan, p. 116. Isaac D'Israeli, in an essay titled "On Vernacular Literature," *New Monthly Magazine*, 34 (1832), 529-40, also concludes with an emphasis on Dante as a language forge, and De Quincey, in an essay on Anglo-Saxon studies (1838) also tropes language formation as metalsmithing (*Collected Works*, 14, p. 151); Blake's Los is of course the most obvious analogy.

37 There seems to be conflicting evidence on the exact nature of this meeting. Browning's letter would seem to place it at Carlyle's house in Cheyne Walk; Carlyle's latest biographer says that Carlyle "met Robert Browning at a party at Leigh Hunt's in early April 1836" (Fred Kaplin, *Thomas Carlyle: A Biography* [Ithaca, New York: Cornell University Press], p. 256); Brown-

ing's latest biographer, however, opens his book with a dramatic first meeting between the two on horseback during one of Carlyle's rides to Wimbledon Common (Donald Thomas, *Robert Browning: A Life Within Life* [New York: The Viking Press, 1982], p. 1). There seems to be no question, though, that Browning was later teased by Carlyle about his dandified appearance.

38 For the correspondence about the bust of Shelley and the Carlyles' season tickets to Covent Garden, see Collected Letters, vol. 9.

39 Lawrence Poston, "Browning's Political Skepticism: *Sordello* and the Plays," *PMLA*, 88 (1973), 260.

40 "Purgatorio," Canto 6, 82-87. *The Divine Comedy of Dante Alighieri: Purgatorio*, trans. Allen Mandelbaum (New York: Bantam Books, 1983), p. 53. Dante's digression on the horrors of warfare is prompted simply by the revelation of the figure's identity as Sordello of Mantua.

41 Browning fills in one of his most artful gaps in 1863, when the line changes from "an evidence / You were... no matter. Let those glances fall!" to "an evidence / You were God: be man now! Let those glances fall!" (V, 96-97).

42 Isobel Armstrong, *Language as Living Form*, p. 141.

43 Hazlitt, "On Thought and Action," in *Table Talk, or Original Essays*, (London: Dent, 1908), p. 101.

44 Bloom's readings of this poem begin with the thesis that at the end there is a swerve (*clinamen*) away from the precursors "where *all* the poets of the Romantic tradition are seen as having failed, to the degree where they stand together": *The Ringers in the Tower: Studies in the Romantic Tradition* (Chicago: University of Chicago Press, 1971), p. 166. Further commentary has come in *A Map of Misreading* (1971), and *Poetry and Repression* (1976).

45 Loy D. Martin's reading of "Pictor Ignotis" is the most thorough; see *Browning's Dramatic Monologues*, p. 35.

46 Benjamin Heath Malkin, *An Introductory Lecture on History, Delivered in the University of London on Thursday, March 11, 1830* (London: 1830), p. 9. Malkin goes on to say that "Innumerable instances of this result are to be found in Sismondi's interesting History of the Italian Republics in the middle ages, and in Mr. Hallam's more general and masterly work embracing the same period."

47 *Browning's Beginnings*, p. 25.

48 *The Complete Poetry and Prose of William Blake*, p. 227 (plate 72).

49 Wordsworth, *Literary Criticism*, p. 54.

50 Erickson, p. 158.

1 James Macpherson, *Poems of Ossian* (New York: 1883), p. 325. For Browning's early reading of Ossian, see John Maynard, *Browning's Youth*, p. 167.

2 Coleridge, *Poetical Works*, p. 406.

3 Blake, p. 127; *Milton*, plate 28.

4 Turner's illustrations to Scott are examined in Gerald Finley's *Landscapes of Memory: Turner as an Illustrator to Scott* (Berkeley: University of California Press, 1981); Turner's frontispiece is reproduced in Jean Clay, *Romanticism*, p. 254.

5 Simonde de Sismondi's two volume *De la littérature du Midi de l'Europe* appeared in 1813; Hazlitt reviewed this work in the Edinburgh Review in 1815, and Thomas Roscoe provided the first English translation in 1823; the work contains detailed chapters on the troubadours and trouveres. Henry Hallam's *View of the State of Europe During the Middle Ages* (2 volumes, 1818) contains a wealth of material on the troubadours and Dante. His four volume *Introduction to the Literature of the Fifteenth, Sixteenth, and Seventeenth Centuries* appeared in 1837-1839. Francis Cary supplied the first complete translation of the *Divine Comedy* in 1814 (his *Inferno* came out in 1805). For the complete list of English versions of Dante during these years, see Gilbert F. Cunningham, *The Divine Comedy in English: A Critical Bibliography*, vol. 1 (Edinburgh and London: Oliver and Boyd, 1965). All of these works, in addition to the French and Italian sources for *Sordello* identified by Stewart Holmes ("The Sources of Browning's *Sordello*," *Studies in Philology*, 34 (1937), 467-96), were assiduously mined for poem, novel, and play throughout the 1830s.

6 Note to *Robert Browning: The Poems*, ed. by John Pettigrew, supplemented and completed by Thomas J. Collins (New Haven: Yale University Press, 1981), 1, p. 1041.

7 [Herman Merivale], "Browning's *Strafford; a Tragedy*," *Edinburgh Review*, 65 (1837), 141. Mary Shelley's *Valperga* offers interesting parallels to *Sordello*, since it is the story of a Prince of Lucca who begins life as a sensitive youth and terminates it as a Machiavellian strongman.

8 See Morse Peckham's chapters on historicism in *Romanticism and Behavior: Collected Essays II*, pp. 32-66.

9 Froula, 978.

10 Karl Kroeber, "Romantic Historicism: The Temporal Sublime," in Kroeber and William Walling, eds., *Images of Romanticism: Verbal and Visual Affinities* (New Haven: Yale University Press, 1978), pp. 164-65. J. Hillis Miller's comments on Browning's historicism are also of interest. See *The Disappearance of God: Five Nineteenth-Century Writers* (New York: Schocken Books, 1965), pp. 106-07.

11 Thomas Weiskel, *The Romantic Sublime: Studies in the Structure of Transcendence* (Baltimore: The Johns Hopkins University Press, 1976), pp. 22-23.

[12] De Quincey, *Works*, VII, p. 251; *Blackwood's* (1844).

[13] Blake, p. 543; from the *Descriptive Catalogue*.

[14] Geoffrey Hartman, *Saving the Text: Literature/Derrida/Philosophy* (Baltimore: The Johns Hopkins University Press, 1981), p. xx.

[15] Lee C. R. Baker, "The Diamond Necklace and the Golden Ring: Historical Imagination in Carlyle and Browning," *Victorian Poetry*, 24 (1986), 44.

[16] Sismondi, *Historical View of the Literature of the South of Europe*, 1, p. 103.

[17] Tucker uses Derrida's wordplay on "difference" to group Browning with Eglamor: "Instead of irritably reaching after conclusive meaning, as Sordello has done throughout his career, Eglamor and Browning choose a secondary stance; in deferring to the future, they preserve an opening in which meaning may grow" (*Browning's Beginnings*, p. 21). My reading of closure in the poem is indebted to Tucker's fine work.

[18] Leigh Hunt, *The Indicator* (London: 1834), 1, p. 84.

[19] For a treatment of the influence of *Sordello* on Pound's *Cantos*, see Ronald Bush, *The Genesis of Ezra Pound's Cantos* (Princeton: Princeton University Press, 1976).

[20] From *Memorials of a Tour on the Continent, 1820*, Wordsworth, *Poetical Works*, p. 273. Mrs. Orr neatly summarizes the import of Rome in her paraphrase of *Sordello*: Rome is "the great constructive power which weaves the past into the future; which represents the continuity of human life," *Handbook*, p. 45.

[21] Frederic Mansel Reynolds, ed., *The Keepsake* (London: 1830), p. 247.

[22] Jerome McGann, in "Rome and Its Romantic Significance," argues that the Romantic myth of Rome culminates in Stendhal's *Rome, Naples, and Florence* (1826); he concludes, "For in Stendhal — and pre-eminently in Stendhal's experience of Rome — the Romantic Movement has summed itself up: has weighed itself in the balances of love and desire, and has found itself, as it had found all other things, finally wanting." *The Beauty of Inflections: Literary Investigations in Historical Method and Theory* (Oxford: Clarendon Press, 1985), p. 333.

[23] Hobhouse's skeptical (and politically liberal) assessment of the sources for much Italian history may be relevant; he notes that "The Guelf and Ghibeline writers are alike unmerciful to popular leaders." *Historical Illustrations of the Fourth Canto of Childe Harold: Containing Dissertations on the Ruins of Rome; and an Essay on Italian Literature*, by John Hobhouse, 2d ed. (London: 1818), 1, p. 253.

[24] Madame de Staël, *Corinne or Italy*, trans. Isabel Hill (New York: Thomas Crowell, 1900), p. 14 and p. 50. De Staël's view of the Italians also sums up Byron's comments, as published in Moore's life. Browning knew de Staël from an early age; one of his two surviving juvenile poems, "The Dance of Death," bears an epigraph from her work.

[25] A. Dwight Culler, *The Victorian Mirror of History* (New Haven: Yale University Press, 1985), p. vi.

26 Philip Kelley and Betty A. Coley, compilers, *The Browning Collections: A Reconstruction With Other Memorabilia* (Winfield, Kansas: The Wedgestone Press, 1984), p. 156; Browning's library also contained an edition of Petrarch's poems published in Parigi in 1829.

27 "Francesco Petrarca," from *The Foreign Quarterly Review*, 1843; *The Complete Works of Walter Savage Landor*, ed. T. Earle Welby (London: Chapman and Hall, 1931), 12, p. 28. Subsequent references cited in the text. Landor's extended "Imaginary Conversation" between Petrarch and Boccaccio, *Pentameron and Pentalogia* was published in 1837. An earlier conversation between the pair appeared in 1829.

28 Edward Bulwer Lytton, *Rienzi: The Last of the Roman Tribunes* (New York: Charles Scribner's Sons, 1903), p. 631. (Appendix I.)

29 Byron, *Selected Poems and Letters*, p. 145 (IV, stanza 114).

30 Hobhouse, 1, p. 256.

31 Byron, *Selected Poems and Letters*, p. 149 (IV, stanza 128).

32 Forster, "Evidences of a New Genius For Dramatic Poetry. —No I," *New Monthly Magazine*, 46 (1836), 302.

33 Shelley, *Poetical Works*, 205. If, as Donald Thomas suggests, Browning aided Moxon in the preparation of the editions of Shelley of 1839 and 1840, he would have had fresh perusals of not only the preface, but Mary Shelley's notes, and in *Essays* many of Shelley's Roman travel letters to Peacock as well, with their detailed descriptions of the ruins and Shelley's reflections on them; *Robert Browning*, p. 87.

NOTES TO CHAPTER FOUR
THE TECHNIQUES OF DIFFICULTY

1 Michael Mason, "The Importance of *Sordello*," in *The Major Victorian Poets: Reconsiderations*, ed. Isobel Armstrong (Lincoln: University of Nebraska Press, 1969), p. 126.

2 William Clyde DeVane, *A Browning Handbook*, p. 81. Clyde de L. Ryals revision of DeVane's account is much more likely; Ryals argues that "when he sat down to begin the writing of the final version Browning was faced with fragments from three prior versions, each conflicting with, each contradicting, the other. . . . How, he must have asked himself, could all this inchoate mass of material be somehow transformed and transmuted into a harmonious union? The answer is that it could not be." Ryals argues that Browning's acceptance of the impossibility of unifying the poem gives him the impetus to swiftly complete his task. *Becoming Browning: The Poems and Plays of Robert Browning, 1833-1846* (Columbus: Ohio State University Press, 1983), p. 69.

3 David Simpson, *Irony and Authority in Romantic Poetry* (Totowa, NJ: Rowman & Littlefield, 1979), p. 190.

4 Ryals, *Becoming Browning*, p. 68. Strangely enough, Margaret Busk's "Modern German School of Irony," *Blackwood's*, 38 (1835), 376-87, is one of the

earliest treatments of "Romantic Irony," though her *Sordello* is one of the least ironic of poems. For an account of the vogue for Sterne and the impact of *Tristram Shandy* on nineteenth-century art, see Peter Conrad's *Shandysim: The Character of Romantic Irony* (New York: Barnes & Noble, 1978). Critics such as William Henry Smith and W. J. Fox attempted to define philosophic or metaphysical character of Romantic poetry; see also Ryals, p. 96, for Browning's description of himself as "Metaphysic Poet."

[5] Thomas R. Lounsbury, *The Early Literary Career of Robert Browning: Four Lectures* (New York: Charles Scribners' Sons, 1911), p. 90. The jungle-clearer as reader is also used by Sterling to describe Carlyle's style in 1839 (Sterling, p. 312).

[6] Edward Dowden, *The Life of Robert Browning* (New York: E. P. Dutton, 1904), p. 35. Dowden in 1867 puts his finger firmly on the stylistic difficulty of *Sordello*, which he says arises not from the much-complained-of mispunctuation (though this amphibolgia is a real problem) but "from the unrelaxing demand which is made throughout upon the intellectual and imaginative energy and alertness of the reader." See "Mr. Browning's *Sordello*," *Fraser's Magazine*, 76 (October, 1867), 518.

[7] Sterling, p. 354.

[8] Tucker, *Browning's Beginnings*, p. 85.

[9] Peterson, "Biblical Typology," p. 244.

[10] James K. Chandler "Romantic Allusiveness," *Critical Inquiry*, 8 (1982), 461-88.

[11] Chandler, "Romantic Allusiveness," 485. See also Ziva Ben-Porat, "The Poetics of Literary Allusion," *PTL*, 1 (1976), 110. Ms Ben-Porat's essay serves as the theoretical basis for one of the few recent attempts to analyze the problem of allusion in Browning, Loy D. Martin's "Browning: The Activation of Influence," *The Victorian Newsletter* (Spring, 1978), 4-9. Among the many distinguished studies of allusion in the eighteenth century, a recent "step towards a grammar of literary allusion" has influenced my analysis here: Robert Folkenflik, "'Homo Alludens' in the Eighteenth Century," *Criticism*, 24 (1982), 218-32.

[12] Horne, *The New Spirit of the Age* (London: Oxford University Press, 1907) p. 378.

[13] A pathfinding example was set by Herbert F. Tucker's "Browning, Eglamor, and Closure in *Sordello*," *Studies in Browning and His Circle*, 4 (1977), 54-70; this close reading of Book VI, 797-819, was also included in *Browning's Beginnings*.

[14] Alan J. Chaffee, "Dialogue and Dialectic in Browning's *Sordello*," 52-77, passim.

[15] DeVane, *Browning's Handbook*, p. 15.

[16] Mrs. Sutherland Orr, *A Handbook to the Works of Robert Browning*, 5th ed. (London: 1890), p. 36.

[17] Shelley, *Poetical Works*, pp. 34-35.

[18] Peter Conrad, *The Victorian Treasure House* (London: Collins, 1973), p. 33.

[19] [Richard Henry Horne], *Spirit of Peers and People. A National Tragi-Comedy* (London: 1834), p. 97.

[20] In *Images of Crisis: Literary Iconology, 1750 to the Present* (Boston: Routledge & Kegan Paul, 1982), George P. Landow comments at length upon the paradigmatic use of the figures of the wreck and deluge in the Romantic period. For the deluge, see pp. 133-44.

[21] See my essay "Shelley's 'Baleful Influence,'" *Studies in Browning and His Circle*, 11 (1983), 31-36, for further discussion of the banishing of Shelley from *Sordello* and Bloom's theory of the anxiety of influence.

[22] For documentation of the impact of Byron on Browning's boyhood, see John Maynard, *Browning's Youth*, pp. 175-77.

[23] John Galt, *Life of Byron*, (London: 1830), p. 238.

[24] Thomas Moore, *Letters and Journals of Lord Byron* (London: 1830), II, p. 404.

[25] In her note to the poems of 1819 in her edition of 1839, Mary Shelley explains Shelley's attempts to take the "people's side" in the inevitable war of the classes by writing poems specifically for them, as well as his "loftier compositions" (Shelley, *Poetical Works*, p. 588).

[26] [Edward Bulwer], "Conversations with an Ambitious Student in Ill-health," *New Monthly Magazine* (1930); rpt. in Edward Bulwer-Lytton, *Miscellaneous Prose Works*, (New York: 1868), 2, p. 284.

[27] Leigh Hunt, *The Indicator*, 2, p. 40.

[28] Paracelsus comes to the realization that it is in the small advance of individual minds, acting in concert with the sea of the people, that progress is made; the metaphor in a speech in *Paracelsus* III (866-79) is similar enough to consider the *Sordello* passage as a revision.

[29] Thomas McFarland, "Field, Constellation, and the Aesthetic Object," *New Literary History*, 13 (1982), 427, 440.

[30] From *De L'esprit de conquête*, quoted and translated by Hugh Honour in *Romanticism* (New York: Harper & Row, 1979), p. 218.

[31] Richard Howitt, *Antediluvian Sketches* (1833); John Heraud, *Judgement of the Flood* (1834); James MacHenry, *The Antediluvians; or The World Destroyed* (1839); and John Edmund Reade, *The Deluge* (1839). The novels are more numerous. In her essay, "John Martin's 'The Deluge,' a Study in Romantic Catastrophe," *Pantheon*, 39 (1981), 220-28, Lynn Matteson provides a wealth of information and describes many of the nineteen deluge paintings exhibited in London between 1775 and 1840. Her essay demonstrates the importance of contemporary biblical criticism and geology (Martin, like Byron, was a supporter of Cuvier) to the growth of the genre, but gives short shrift to the political metaphor. Byron's "mystery" *Heaven and Earth* (1821), which ends with the coming of the deluge, was quoted by John Martin in the pamphlet that accompanied the exhibition of his painting in 1826.

[32] Danby's picture is described in Landow, p. 140 and pl. 14.

145

[33] [Edward Bulwer], "On the Difference Between Authors and the Impression of them Conveyed by their Works," *New Monthly Magazine* (1832); rpt. *Miscellaneous Prose Works*, 2, p. 11.

[34] See Paul Ricouer, "The Metaphorical Process as Cognition, Imagination, and Feeling," in *On Metaphor*, ed. Sheldon Sacks (Chicago: University of Chicago Press, 1979), pp. 141-60. Much of what Ricouer theorizes about the connection of imagination and feeling in metaphor fits in with Browning's Romantic use of figures in Sordello.

[35] Donald S. Hair seems to believe that one of the audience pipes in with "Fool..." rather than the narrator; *Browning's Experiments with Genre* (Toronto: University of Toronto Press, 1972), p. 31. I think that this is wrong, though we both may be victims of playing Browning's game of "who speaks here?"

[36] Tucker, *Browning's Beginning's*, p. 23.

[37] Dowden, "Mr. Browning's *Sordello*," 519.

[38] Erickson (p. 42) also notes the impact of Macready on Browning's style.

[39] Tucker, *Browning's Beginning's*, p. 101.

[40] Sterne, *Tristram Shandy*, p. 83.

[41] Stempel, "Browning's *Sordello*: The Art of the Makers-see," 559.

[42] Robert A. Lecker, "The Crisis of Meeting: Mediation and Synthesis in Browning's *Sordello*," *English Studies in Canada*, 3 (1977), 308. Clyde de L. Ryals points out how "even this new kind of poetry, although it will allow more to be expressed than ever before, will prove inadequate to deal not only with all human experience but also with what the poet himself wants to say" ("Browning's Irony," p. 34).

[43] Letter to Coleridge (1797), in *The Works of Charles and Mary Lamb*, ed. E. V. Lucas (London: 1903), 6, p. 76.

[44] Hallam, *Writings*, p. 143.

NOTES TO EPILOGUE
"PIPPA PASSES"

[1] W. Hall Griffin & Harry Christopher Minchin, *The Life of Robert Browning, With Notices of His Writings, His Family, & His Friends* (1910; Hamden, CT: Archon Books, 1966), pp. 125-126.

[2] Ryals, *Becoming Browning*, p. 120.

[3] Orr, p. 56.

[4] Representative readings of the poem that focus on its irony may be found in E. Warwick Slinn, *Browning and the Fictions of Identity* (London: Macmillan, 1982), Clyde de L. Ryals, *Becoming Browning*, and Herbert F. Tucker, *Browning's Beginnings*.

[5] Lawrence Poston, III, "Browning's Political Skepticism: *Sordello* and the Plays," *PMLA*, 88 (1973), 264.

[6] Samuel L. Chell, *The Dynamic Self: Browning's Poetry of Duration* (Victoria, BC: ELS Monograph Series, no. 32, 1984), p. 55.

[7] Michael Mason, "The Importance of *Sordello*," p. 143. Armstrong reads this passage as an utterance of Plara, but this is not necessarily the case, as a comparison with the sample of Plara's verse in Book II shows.

[8] Fleishman, *Genre*, 18 (1985), 365.

[9] Sterling, p. 274.

[10] Friedrich von Schiller, *Naive and Sentimental Poetry and On the Sublime: Two Essays*, trans. Julius A. Elias (New York: Ungar, 1966), pp. 98-99. Michael Mason believes that "The whole notion of literary progress in *Sordello* speaks sharply and consistently of the kind of German romantic view that is best expressed in Schiller's 'Uber naive und sentimentalische Dichtung'" (p. 143), and he reviews the various ways through which Browning might have been exposed to German thoughts on poetry.

[11] Lawrence Poston, for instance, says that "read in the context of Browning's developing aims as a poet, the latter day of "the barefoot and rosy child" seems to prefigure that New Year's Day, also at Asolo, when the girl from the silk-mills rises to greet the dawn." "Browning's Career to 1841: The Theme of Time and the problem of Form," *Browning Institute Studies*, 3 (1975), 93-94.

[12] Mill, *Literary Essays*, p. 56; Ryals suggests that Browning questions his own poetic career through *Pippa*: "What if he had become the kind of poet that J. S. Mill wanted all poets to be, a singer overheard" —*Becoming Browning*, p. 120.

147

Printed in the USA
CPSIA information can be obtained
at www.ICGtesting.com
LVHW010053110224
771468LV00017B/245